BASIL BLACKWELL, OXFORD
JOHNSON REPRINT CORPORATION, NEW YORK

1973

*Library of Congress Cataloging in Publication Data:*

Pater, Walter Horatio, 1839-1894.
Essays from 'The Guardian.'

CONTENTS: English literature.—Amiel's "Journal intime."
—Browning. [etc.]
1. English literature—19th century—Addresses, essays, lectures.
2. French literature—19th century—Addresses, essays, lectures. I. Title.
PR5134.E7 1973 809 72-10895
ISBN 0-384-45090-3

Reprinted with the permission of the original publisher
First reprinting, 1967
Second reprinting, 1973

Johnson Reprint Corporation, 111 Fifth Avenue, New York, New York 10003
Basil Blackwell, Broad Street, Oxford, England
Printed in the United States of America

Essays from 'The Guardian'

MACMILLAN AND CO., LIMITED
LONDON · BOMBAY · CALCUTTA
MELBOURNE

THE MACMILLAN COMPANY
NEW YORK · BOSTON · CHICAGO
ATLANTA · SAN FRANCISCO

THE MACMILLAN CO. OF CANADA, LTD.
TORONTO

# ESSAYS

FROM

# 'THE GUARDIAN'

BY

WALTER PATER

MACMILLAN AND CO., LIMITED
ST. MARTIN'S STREET, LONDON
1910

*First published (Edition de Luxe) August* 1901
*Reprinted September* 1901
*Reprinted (Extra Crown 8vo)* 1903, 1906
*Library Edition* 1910

# NOTE

THE nine papers contained in the following volume originally appeared anonymously in *The Guardian* newspaper.

# CONTENTS

# I

# ENGLISH LITERATURE

17TH FEBRUARY 1886

# ENGLISH LITERATURE

## Four Books for Students of English Literature

The making of an anthology of English prose is what must have occurred to many of its students, by way of pleasure to themselves, or of profit to other persons. Such an anthology, the compass and variety of our prose literature being considered, might well follow exclusively some special line of interest in it; exhibiting, for instance, what is so obviously striking, its imaginative power, or its (legitimately) poetic beauty, or again, its philosophical capacity. Mr. Saintsbury's well-considered *Specimens of English Prose Style, from Malory to Macaulay* (Kegan Paul), a volume, as we think, which bears fresh witness to the truth of the old remark that it takes a scholar indeed to make a good literary selection, has its motive sufficiently indicated in the very original "introductory essay," which might well stand, along with the best of these extracts from a hundred or more deceased masters of English, as itself a document or standard, in the matter of prose style. The essential difference between poetry and prose—"that other beauty of prose"—in the words of the motto he has chosen from Dryden, the first master of the sort of prose he prefers:—that is Mr. Saintsbury's burden. It is a consideration, undoubtedly, of great importance both for the writer and the critic; in England especially, where, although (as Mr. Saintsbury rightly points out, in correction of an imperfectly informed French critic of our literature) the radical distinction between poetry and prose has ever been recognized by its students, yet the imaginative impulse, which is perhaps the richest of our purely intellectual gifts, has been apt to invade the province of that tact and good judgment, alike as to matter and manner, in which we are not richer than other people. Great poetry and great prose, it might be found, have most of their qualities in common. But their indispensable qualities are different, or even opposed; and it is just the indispensable qualities of prose and poetry respectively, which it is so necessary for those who have to do with either to bear ever in mind. Order, precision, directness, are the radical merits of prose thought; and it is more than merely legitimate that they should form the criterion of prose style, because within the scope of those qualities, according to Mr. Saintsbury, there is more than just the quiet, unpretending usefulness of the bare *sermo pedestris*. Acting on language, those qualities generate a specific and unique beauty—"that other beauty of prose"—fitly illustrated by these specimens, which the reader needs hardly be told, after what has been now said, are far from being a collection of "purple patches."

Whether or not he admits their practical cogency, an attentive reader will not fail to be interested in the attempt Mr. Saintsbury has made to give technical rules of metre for the production of the true prose rhythm. Any one who cares to do so might test the validity of those rules in the nearest possible way, by applying them to the varied examples in this wide survey of what has been actually well done in English prose, here exhibited on the side of their strictly prosaic merit—their conformity, before all other aims, to laws of a structure primarily reasonable. Not that that reasonable prose structure, or architecture, as Mr. Saintsbury conceives it, has been always, or even generally, the ideal, even of those chosen writers here in evidence. Elizabethan prose, all too chaotic in the beauty and force which overflowed into it from Elizabethan poetry, and incorrect with an incorrectness which leaves it scarcely legitimate prose at all: then, in reaction against that, the correctness of Dryden, and his followers through the eighteenth century, determining the standard of a prose in the proper sense, not inferior to the prose of the Augustan age in Latin, or of the "great age in France": and, again in reaction against this, the wild mixture of poetry and prose, in our wild nineteenth century, under the influence of such writers as Dickens and Carlyle: —such are the three periods into which the story of our prose literature divides itself. And Mr. Saintsbury has his well-timed, practical suggestions, upon a survey of them.

ENGLISH LITERATURE

If the invasion of the legitimate sphere of prose in England by the spirit of poetry, weaker or stronger, has been something far deeper than is indicated by that tendency to write unconscious blank verse, which has made it feasible to transcribe about one-half of Dickens's otherwise so admirable *Barnaby Rudge* in blank-verse lines, a tendency (outdoing our old friend M. Jourdain) commoner than Mr. Saintsbury admits, such lines being frequent in his favourite Dryden; yet, on the other hand, it might be maintained, and would be maintained by its French critics, that our English poetry has been too apt to dispense with those prose qualities, which, though not the indispensable qualities of poetry, go, nevertheless, to the making of all first-rate poetry—the qualities, namely, of orderly structure, and such qualities generally as depend upon second thoughts. A collection of specimens of English poetry, for the purpose of exhibiting the achievement of prose excellences by it (in their legitimate measure) is a *desideratum* we commend to Mr. Saintsbury. It is the assertion, the development, the product of those very different indispensable qualities of poetry, in the presence of which the English is equal or superior to all other modern literature—the native, sublime, and beautiful, but often wild and irregular, imaginative power in English poetry from Chaucer to Shakespeare, with which Professor Minto deals, in his *Characteristics of English Poets* (Blackwood), lately reprinted. That his book should have found many readers we can well understand, in the light of the excellent qualities which, in high degree, have gone to the making of it: a tasteful learning, never deserted by that hold upon contemporary literature which is so animating an influence in the study of what belongs to the past. Beginning with an elaborate notice of Chaucer, full of the minute scholarship of our day, he never forgets that his subject is, after all, poetry. The followers of Chaucer, and the precursors of Shakespeare, are alike real persons to him—old Langland reminding him of Carlyle's "Gospel of Labour." The product of a large store of reading has been here secreted anew for the reader who desires to see, in bird's-eye view, the light and shade of a long and varied period of poetic literature, by way of preparation for Shakespeare, (with a full essay upon whom the volume closes,) explaining Shakespeare, so far as he can be explained by literary antecedents.

That powerful poetry was twin-brother to a prose, of more varied, but certainly of wilder and more irregular power than the admirable, the typical, prose of Dryden. In Dryden, and his followers through the eighteenth century, we see the reaction against the exuberance and irregularity of that prose, no longer justified by power, but cognizable rather as bad taste. But such reaction was effective only because an age had come—the age of a negative, or agnostic philosophy—in which men's minds must needs be limited to the superficialities of things, with a kind of narrowness amounting to a positive gift. What that mental attitude was capable of, in the way of an elegant, yet plain-spoken, and life-like delineation of men's moods and manners, as also in the way of determining those moods and manners themselves to all that was lively, unaffected, and harmonious, can be seen nowhere better than in Mr. Austin Dobson's *Selections from Steele* (Clarendon Press) prefaced by his careful "Life." The well-known qualities of

Mr. Dobson's own original work are a sufficient guarantee of the taste and discrimination we may look for in a collection like this, in which the random lightnings of the first of the essayists are grouped under certain heads—"Character Sketches," "Tales and Incidents," "Manners and Fashions," and the like—so as to diminish, for the general reader, the scattered effect of short essays on a hundred various subjects, and give a connected, book-like character to the specimens.

Steele, for one, had certainly succeeded in putting himself, and his way of taking the world—for this pioneer of an everybody's literature had his subjectivities—into books. What a survival of one long-past day, for instance, in "A Ramble from Richmond to London"! What truth to the surface of common things, to their direct claim on our interest! yet with what originality of effect in that truthfulness, when he writes, for instance:

"I went to my lodgings, led by a light, whom I put into the discourse of his private economy, and made him give me an account of the charge, hazard, profit, and loss of a family that depended upon a link."

It was one of his peculiarities, he tells us, to live by the eye far more than by any other sense (a peculiarity, perhaps, in an Englishman), and this is what he sees at the early daily service then common in some City churches. Among those who were come only to see or be seen, "there were indeed a few in whose looks there appeared a heavenly joy and gladness upon the entrance of a new day, as if they had gone to sleep with expectation of it."

The industrious reader, indeed, might select out of these specimens from Steele, a picture, in minute detail, of the characteristic manners of that time. Still, beside, or only a little way beneath, such a picture of passing fashion, what Steele and his fellows really deal with is the least transitory aspects of life, though still merely aspects — those points in which all human nature, great or little, finds what it has in common, and directly shows itself up. The natural strength of such literature will, of course, be in the line of its tendencies; in transparency, variety, and directness. To the unembarrassing matter, the unembarrassed style! Steele is, perhaps, the most impulsive writer of the school to which he belongs; he abounds in felicities of impulse. Yet who can help feeling that his style is regular because the matter he deals with is the somewhat uncontentious, even, limited soul, of an age not imaginative, and unambitious in its speculative flight? Even in Steele himself we may observe with what sureness of instinct the men of that age turned aside at the contact of anything likely to make them, in any sense, forget themselves.

No one indicates better than Charles Lamb, to whose memory Mr. Alfred Ainger has done such good service, the great and peculiar change which was begun at the end of the last century, and dominates our own; that sudden increase of the width, the depth, the complexity of intellectual interest, which has many times torn and distorted literary style, even with those best able to comprehend its laws. In *Mrs. Leicester's School, with other Writings in Prose and Verse* (Macmillan), Mr. Ainger has collected and annotated certain remains of Charles and Mary Lamb, too good to lie unknown to the present generation, in forgotten periodicals or inaccessible reprints. The story of the Odyssey, abbreviated in very simple prose, for children—of all ages—will speak for itself. But the garland of graceful stories which gives name to the volume, told by a party of girls on the evening of their assembling at school, are in the highest degree characteristic of the brother and sister who were ever so successful in imparting to others their own enjoyment of books and people. The tragic circumstance which strengthened and consecrated their natural community of interest had, one might think, something to do with the far-reaching pensiveness even of their most humorous writing, touching often the deepest springs of pity and awe, as the way of the highest humour is—a way, however, very different from that of the humorists of the eighteenth century. But one cannot forget also that Lamb was early an enthusiastic admirer of Wordsworth: of Wordsworth, the first characteristic power of the nineteenth century, his essay on whom, in the *Quarterly Review*, Mr. Ainger here reprints. Would that he could have reprinted it as originally composed, and ungarbled by Gifford, the editor! Lamb, like Wordsworth, still kept the charm of a serenity, a precision, unsurpassed by the quietest essayist of the preceding age. But it might have been foreseen that the rising tide of thought and feeling, on the strength of which they too are borne upward, would sometimes overflow barriers. And so it happens that these simple stories are touched, much as Wordsworth's verse-stories were, with tragic power. Dealing with the beginnings of imagination in the minds of children, they record, with the reality which a very delicate touch preserves from anything lugubrious, not those merely preventible miseries of childhood over which some writers have been apt to gloat, but the contact of childhood with the great and inevitable sorrows of life, into which children can enter with depth, with dignity, and sometimes with a kind of simple, pathetic greatness, to the discipline of the heart. Let the reader begin with the "Sea Voyage," which is by Charles Lamb; and, what Mr. Ainger especially recommends, the "Father's Wedding-Day," by his sister Mary.

The ever-increasing intellectual burden of our age is hardly likely to adapt itself to the exquisite, but perhaps too delicate and limited, literary instruments of the age of Queen Anne. Yet Mr. Saintsbury is certainly right in thinking that, as regards style, English literature has much to do. Well, the good quality of an age, the defect of which lies in the direction of intellectual anarchy and confusion, may well be eclecticism: in style, as in other things, it is well always to aim at the combination of as many excellences as possible—opposite excellences, it may be—those other *beauties* of prose. A busy age will hardly educate its writers in correctness. Let its writers make time to write English more as a learned language; and completing that correction of style which had only gone a certain way in the last century, raise the general level of language towards their own. If there be a weakness in Mr. Saintsbury's view, it is perhaps in a tendency to regard style a little too independently of matter. And there are still some who think that, after all, the style is the man; justified, in very great varieties, by the simple consideration of what he himself has to say, quite independently of any real or supposed connection with this or that literary age or school. Let us close with the words of a most versatile master of English — happily not yet included in Mr. Saintsbury's book — a writer who has dealt with all the perturbing influences of our century in a manner as classical, as idiomatic, as easy and elegant, as Steele's :

"I wish you to observe," says Cardinal Newman, "that the mere dealer in words cares little or nothing for the subject which he is embellishing, but can paint and gild anything whatever to order ; whereas the artist, whom I am acknowledging, has his great or rich visions before him, and his only aim is to bring out what he thinks or what he feels in a way adequate to the thing spoken of, and appropriate to the speaker."

II

# AMIEL'S "JOURNAL INTIME"

17TH MARCH 1886

## AMIEL'S "JOURNAL INTIME"

*Amiel's Journal.* The *Journal Intime* of Henri-Frédéric Amiel. Translated, with an Introduction and Notes, by Mrs. Humphry Ward. Two vols. Macmillans.

CERTAIN influential expressions of opinion have attracted much curiosity to Amiel's *Journal Intime*, both in France, where the book has already made its mark, and in England, where Mrs. Humphry Ward's translation is likely to make it widely known among all serious lovers of good literature. Easy, idiomatic, correct, this English version reads like an excellent original English work, and gives fresh proof that the work of translation, if it is to be done with effect, must be done by those who, possessing, like Mrs. Ward, original literary gifts, are willing to make a long act of self-denial or self-effacement for the benefit of the public. In this case, indeed, the work is not wholly one of self-effacement, for the accomplished translator has prefaced *Amiel's Journal* by an able and interesting essay of seventy pages on Amiel's life and intellectual position. And certainly there is much in the book, thus effectively presented to the English reader, to attract those who interest themselves in the study of the finer types of human nature, of literary expression, of metaphysical and practical philosophy; to attract, above all, those interested in such philosophy, at points where it touches upon questions of religion, and especially at the present day.

Henri-Frédéric Amiel was born at Geneva in 1821. Orphaned of both his parents at the age of twelve, his youth was necessarily "a little bare and forlorn," and a deep interest in religion became fixed in him early. His student days coming to an end, the years which followed, from 1842 to 1848—*Wanderjahre*, in which he visited Holland, Italy, Sicily, and the principal towns of Germany—seem to have been the happiest of his life. In 1849 he became a Professor at Geneva, and there is little more to tell of him in the way of outward events. He published some volumes of verse ; to the last apparently still only feeling after his true literary *métier*. Those last seven years were a long struggle against the disease which ended his life, consumption, at the age of fifty-three. The first entry in his *Journal* is in 1848. From that date to his death, a period of over twenty-five years, this *Journal* was the real object of all the energies of his richly-endowed nature: and from its voluminous sheets his literary executors have selected the deeply interesting volumes now presented in English.

With all its gifts and opportunities it was a melancholy life—melancholy with something not altogether explained by the somewhat pessimistic philosophy exposed in the *Journal*, nor by the consumptive tendency of Amiel's physical constitution, causing him from a very early date to be much preoccupied with the effort to reconcile himself with the prospect of death, and reinforcing the far from sanguine temperament of one intellectually also a *poitrinaire*.

You might think him at first sight only an admirable specimen of a thoroughly well-educated man, full, of course, of the modern spirit ; stimulated and formed by the influences of the varied intellectual world around him ; and competing, in his turn, with many very various types of contemporary ability. The use of his book to cultivated people might lie in its affording a kind of standard by which they might take measure of the maturity and producible quality of their own thoughts on a hundred important subjects. He will write a page or two, giving evidence of that accumulated power and attainment which, with a more strenuous temperament, might have sufficed for an effective volume. Continually, in the *Journal*, we pause over things that would rank for beauties among widely differing models of the best French prose. He has said some things in Pascal's vein not unworthy of Pascal. He had a right to compose "Thoughts" : they have the force in them which makes up for their unavoidable want of continuity.

But if, as Amiel himself challenges us to do, we look below the surface of a very equable and even smoothly accomplished literary manner, we discover, in high degree of development, that perplexity or complexity of soul, the expression of which, so it be with an adequate literary gift, has its legitimate, because inevitable, interest for the modern reader. Senancour and Maurice de Guérin in one, seem to have been supplemented here by a larger experience, a far greater education, than either of them had attained to. So multiplex is the result that minds of quite opposite type might well discover in these pages their own special thought or humour, happily expressed at last (they might think) in precisely that just shade of language themselves had searched for in vain. And with a writer so vivid and impressive as Amiel, those varieties of tendency are apt to present themselves as so many contending persons. The perplexed experience gets the apparent clearness, as it gets also the animation, of a long dialogue; only, the disputants never part company, and there is no real conclusion. "This nature," he observes, of one of the many phases of character he has discovered in himself, "is, as it were, only one of the men which exist in me. It is one of my departments. It is not the whole of my territory, the whole of my inner kingdom"; and again, "there are ten men in me, according to time, place, surrounding, and occasion ; and, in my restless diversity, I am for ever escaping myself."

Yet, in truth, there are but two men in Amiel —two sufficiently opposed personalities, which the attentive reader may define for himself ; compare with, and try by each other—as we think, correct also by each other. There is the man, in him and in these pages, who would be "the man of disillusion," only that he has never really been "the man of desires" ; and who seems, therefore, to have a double weariness about him. He is akin, of course, to Obermann, to René, even to Werther, and, on our first introduction to him, we might think that we had to do only with one more of the vague "renunciants," who in real life followed those creations of fiction, and who, however delicate, interesting as a study, and as it were picturesque on the stage of life, are themselves, after all, essentially passive, uncreative, and therefore necessarily not of first-rate importance in literature. Taken for what it is worth, the expression of this mood—the culture of *ennui* for its own sake—is certainly carried to its ideal of negation by Amiel. But the completer, the positive, soul, which will merely take that mood into its service (its proper service, as we hold, is in counteraction to the vulgarity of purely positive natures) is also certainly in evidence in Amiel's "Thoughts"—that other, and far stronger person, in the long dialogue; the man, in short, possessed of gifts, not for the renunciation, but for the reception and use, of all that is puissant, goodly, and effective in life, and for the varied and adequate literary reproduction of it; who, under favourable circumstances, or even without them, will become critic, or poet, and in either case a creative force; and if he be religious (as Amiel was deeply religious) will make the most of "evidence," and almost certainly find a Church.

The sort of purely poetic tendency in his mind, which made Amiel known in his own lifetime chiefly as a writer of verse, seems to be represented in these volumes by certain passages of natural description, always sincere, and sometimes rising to real distinction. In Switzerland it is easy to be pleased with scenery. But the record of such pleasure becomes really worth while when, as happens with Amiel, we feel that there has been, and with success, an intellectual effort to get at the secret, the precise motive, of the pleasure ; to *define* feeling, in this matter. Here is a good description of an effect of fog, which we commend to foreigners resident in London :

"Fog has certainly a poetry of its own—a grace, a dreamy charm. It does for the daylight what a lamp does for us at night ; it turns the mind towards meditation ; it throws the soul back on itself. The sun, as it were, sheds us abroad in nature, scatters and disperses us ; mist draws us together and concentrates us—it is cordial, homely, charged with feeling. The poetry of the sun has something of the epic in it ; that of fog and mist is elegiac and religious. Pantheism is the child of light ; mist engenders faith in near protectors. When the great world is shut off from us, the house becomes itself a small universe. Shrouded in perpetual mist, men love each other better ; for the only reality then is the family, and, within the family, the heart ; and the greatest thoughts come from the heart—so says the moralist."

It is of Swiss fog, however, that he is speaking, as, in what follows, of Swiss frost :

"Three snowstorms this afternoon. Poor blossoming plum-trees and peach-trees! What a difference from six years ago, when the cherry-trees, adorned in their green spring dress and laden with their bridal flowers, smiled at my departure along the Vaudois fields, and the lilacs of Burgundy threw great gusts of perfume into my face!" The weather is seldom talked of with so much real sensitiveness to it as in this:

"The weather is rainy, the whole atmosphere grey; it is a time favourable to thought and meditation. I have a liking for such days as these; they revive one's converse with oneself and make it possible to live the inner life: they are quiet and peaceful, like a song in a minor key. We are nothing but thought, but we feel our life to its very centre. Our very sensations turn to reverie. It is a strange state of mind; it is like those silences in worship which are not the empty moments of devotion, but the full moments, and which are so because at such times the soul, instead of being polarized, dispersed, localized, in a single impression or thought, feels her own totality and is conscious of herself."

"Every landscape," he writes, "is, as it were, a state of the soul": and again, "At bottom there is but one subject of study; the forms and metamorphoses of mind: all other subjects may be reduced to that; all other studies bring us back to this study." And, in truth, if he was occupied with the aspects of nature to such an excellent literary result, still, it was with nature only as a phenomenon of the moral order. His interest, after all, is, consistently, that of the moralist (in no narrow sense) who deals, from predilection, with the sort of literary work which *stirs* men—stirs their intellect—through feeling; and with that literature, especially, as looked at through the means by which it became capable of thus commanding men. The powers, the culture, of the literary producer: there, is the centre of Amiel's curiosity.

And if we take Amiel at his own word, we must suppose that but for causes, the chief of which were bad health and a not long life, he too would have produced monumental work, whose scope and character he would wish us to conjecture from his "Thoughts." Such indications there certainly are in them. He was meant—we see it in the variety, the high level both of matter and style, the animation, the gravity, of one after another of these thoughts—on religion, on poetry, on politics in the highest sense; on their most abstract principles, and on the authors who have given them a personal colour; on the genius of those authors, as well as on their concrete works; on outlying isolated subjects, such as music, and special musical composers—he was meant, if people ever are meant for special lines of activity, for the best sort of criticism, the imaginative criticism; that criticism which is itself a kind of construction, or creation, as it penetrates, through the given literary or artistic product, into the mental and inner constitution of the producer, shaping his work. Of such critical skill, cultivated with all the resources of Geneva in the nineteenth century, he has given in this *Journal* abundant proofs. Corneille, Cherbuliez; Rousseau, Sismondi; Victor Hugo, and Joubert; Mozart and Wagner—all who are interested in these men will find a value in what Amiel has to say of them. Often, as for instance in his excellent criticism of Quinet, he has to make large exceptions; limitations, skilfully effected by the way, in the course of a really appreciative estimate. Still, through all, what we feel is that we have to do with one who criticises in this fearlessly equitable manner only because he is convinced that his subject is of a real literary importance. A powerful, intellectual analysis of some well-marked subject, in such form as makes literature enduring, is indeed what the world might have looked for from him: those institutes of æsthetics, for instance, which might exist, after Lessing and Hegel, but which certainly do not exist yet. "Construction," he says—artistic or literary construction—"rests upon feeling, instinct, and," alas! also, "upon will." The instinct, at all events, was certainly his. And over and above that he had possessed himself of the art of expressing, in quite natural language, very difficult thoughts; those abstract and metaphysical conceptions especially, in which German mind has been rich, which are bad masters, but very useful ministers towards the understanding, towards an analytical survey, of all that the intellect has produced.

But something held him back: not so much

a reluctancy of temperament, or of physical constitution (common enough cause why men of undeniable gifts fail of commensurate production) but a cause purely intellectual—the presence in him, namely, of a certain vein of opinion; that other, constituent but contending, person, in his complex nature. "The relation of thought to action," he writes, "filled my mind on waking, and I found myself carried towards a bizarre formula, which seems to have something of the night still clinging about it. *Action is but coarsened thought.*" That is but an ingenious metaphysical point, as he goes on to show. But, including in "action" that literary production in which the line of his own proper activity lay, he followed—followed often—that fastidious utterance to a cynical and pessimistic conclusion. *Maia*, as he calls it, the empty "Absolute" of the Buddhist, the "Infinite," the "All," of which those German metaphysicians he loved only too well have had so much to say: this was for ever to give the go-by to all positive, finite, limited interests whatever. The vague pretensions of an abstract expression acted on him with all the force of a prejudice. "The ideal," he admits, "poisons for me all imperfect possession"; and again, "The Buddhist tendency in me blunts the faculty of free self-government, and weakens the power of action. I feel a terror of action and am only at ease in the impersonal, disinterested, and objective line of thought." But then, again, with him "action" meant chiefly literary production. He quotes with approval those admirable words from Goethe, "In der Beschränkung zeigt sich erst der Meister"; yet still always finds himself wavering between "frittering myself away on the infinitely little, and longing after what is unknown and distant." There is, doubtless, over and above the physical consumptive tendency, an instinctive turn of sentiment in this touching confession. Still, what strengthened both tendencies was that metaphysical prejudice for the "Absolute," the false intellectual conscience. "I have always avoided what attracted me, and turned my back upon the point where secretly I desired to be"; and, of course, that is not the way to a free and generous productivity, in literature, or in anything else; though in literature, with Amiel at all events, it meant the fastidiousness which is incompatible with any but the very best sort of production.

And as that abstract condition of *Maia*, to the kind and quantity of concrete literary production we hold to have been originally possible for him; so was the religion he actually attained, to what might have been the development of his profoundly religious spirit, had he been able to see that the old-fashioned Christianity is itself but the proper historic development of the true "essence" of the New Testament. There, again, is the constitutional shrinking, through a kind of metaphysical prejudice, from the concrete—that fear of the actual—in this case, of the Church of history; to which the admissions, which form so large a part of these volumes, naturally lead. Assenting, on probable evidence, to so many of the judgments of the religious sense, he failed to see the equally probable evidence there is for the beliefs, the peculiar direction of men's hopes, which complete those judgments harmoniously, and bring them into connection with the facts, the venerable institutions of the past—with the lives of the saints. By failure, as we think, of that historic sense, of which he could speak so well, he got no further in this direction than the glacial condition of rationalistic Geneva. "Philosophy," he says, "can never replace religion." Only, one cannot see why it might not replace a religion such as his: a religion, after all, much like Seneca's. "I miss something," he himself confesses, "common worship, a positive religion, shared with other people. Ah! when will the Church to which I belong in heart rise into being?" To many at least of those who can detect the ideal through the disturbing circumstances which belong to all actual institutions in the world, it was already there. Pascal, from considerations to which Amiel was no stranger, came to the large hopes of the Catholic Church; Amiel stopped short at a faith almost hopeless; and by stopping short just there he really failed, as we think, of intellectual consistency, and missed that appeasing influence which his nature demanded as the condition of its full activity, as a force, an intellectual force, in the world—in the special business of his life. "Welcome the unforeseen," he says again, by way of a counsel of perfection in the matter of culture, "but give to your life unity, and bring the unforeseen within the lines of your plan." Bring, we should add, the Great Possibility at least within the lines of your plan—your plan of action or production; of morality; especially of your conceptions of religion. And still, Amiel too, be it remembered (we are not afraid to repeat it), has said some things in Pascal's vein not unworthy of Pascal.

And so we get only the *Journal*. Watching in it, in the way we have suggested, the contention of those two men, those two minds in him, and observing how the one might have ascertained and corrected the shortcomings of the other, we certainly understand, and can sympathize with Amiel's despondency in the retrospect of a life which seemed to have been but imperfectly occupied. But, then, how excellent a literary product, after all, the *Journal* is. And already we have found that it improves also on second reading. A book of "thoughts" should be a book that may be fairly dipped into, and yield good quotable sayings. Here are some of its random offerings:

"Look twice, if what you want is a just

conception; look once, if what you want is a sense of beauty."

"It is not history which teaches conscience to be honest; it is the conscience which educates history. Fact is corrupting—it is we who correct it by the persistence of our ideal."

"To do easily what is difficult for others is the mark of talent. To do what is impossible for talent is the mark of genius."

"Duty has the virtue of making us feel the reality of a positive world, while at the same time detaching us from it."

"As it is impossible to be outside God, the best is consciously to dwell in Him."

"He also (the Son of Man), He above all, is the great Misunderstood, the least comprehended."

"The *pensée* writer is to the philosopher what the *dilettante* is to the artist."

There are some, we know, who hold that genius cannot, in the nature of things, be "sterile"; that there are no "mute" Miltons, or the like. Well! genius, or only a very distinguished talent, the gift which Amiel nursed so jealously did come into evidence. And the reader, we hope, sees also already how well his English translator has done her work. She may justly feel, as part at least of the reward of a labour which must have occupied much time, so many of the freshest hours of mind and spirit, that she has done something to help her author in the achievement of his, however discouraged still irrepressible, desire, by giving additional currency to a book which the best sort of readers will recognize as an excellent and certainly very versatile companion, not to be forgotten.

# III

# BROWNING

9TH NOVEMBER 1887

# BROWNING

*An Introduction to the Study of Browning.*
By Arthur Symons. Cassells.

WHETHER it be true or not that Mr. Browning is justly chargeable with "obscurity"—with a difficulty of manner, that is, beyond the intrinsic difficulty of his matter—it is very probable that an Introduction to the study of his works, such as this of Mr. Symons, will add to the number of his readers. Mr. Symons's opening essay on the general characteristics of Mr. Browning is a just and acceptable appreciation of his poetry as a whole, well worth reading, even at this late day. We find in Mr. Symons the thoughtful and practised yet enthusiastic student in literature—in intellectual problems; always quiet and sane, praising Mr. Browning with tact, with a real refinement and grace; saying well many things which every competent reader of the great poet must feel to be true; devoting to the subject he loves a critical gift so considerable as to make us wish for work from his hands of larger scope than this small volume. His book is, according to his intention, before all things a useful one. Appreciating Mr. Browning fairly, as we think, in all his various efforts, his aim is to point his readers to the best, the indisputable, rather than to the dubious portions of his author's work. Not content with his own excellent general criticism of Mr. Browning, he guides the reader to his works, or division of work, *seriatim*, making of each a distinct and special study, and giving a great deal of welcome information about the poems, the circumstances of their composition, and the like, with delightful quotations. Incidentally, his Introduction has the interest of a brief but effective selection from Mr. Browning's poems; and he has added an excellent biography.

Certainly we shall not quarrel with Mr. Symons for reckoning Mr. Browning, among English poets, second to Shakespeare alone—"He comes very near the gigantic total of

Shakespeare." The *quantity* of his work? Yes! that too, in spite of a considerable unevenness, is a sign of genius. "So large, indeed, appear to be his natural endowments that we cannot feel as if even thirty volumes would have come near to exhausting them." Imaginatively, indeed, Mr. Browning has been a multitude of persons; only (as Shakespeare's only untried style was the simple one) almost never simple ones; and certainly he has controlled them all to profoundly interesting artistic ends by his own powerful personality. The world and all its action, as a show of thought, that is the scope of his work. It makes him pre-eminently a modern poet—a poet of the self-pondering, perfectly educated, modern world, which, having come to the end of all direct and purely external experiences, must necessarily turn for its entertainment to the world within:—

"The men and women who live and move in that new world of his creation are as varied as life itself; they are kings and beggars, saints and lovers, great captains, poets, painters, musicians, priests and Popes, Jews, gipsies and dervishes, street-girls, princesses, dancers with the wicked witchery of the daughter of Herodias, wives with the devotion of the wife of Brutus, joyous girls and malevolent grey-beards, statesmen, cavaliers, soldiers of humanity, tyrants and bigots, ancient sages and modern spiritualists, heretics, scholars, scoundrels, devotees, rabbis, persons of quality and men of low estate—men and women as multiform as nature or society has made them."

The individual, the personal, the concrete, as distinguished from, yet revealing in its fulness, the general, the universal—that is Mr. Browning's chosen subject-matter :—"Every man is for him an epitome of the universe, a centre of creation." It is always the particular soul, and the particular act or episode, as the flower of the particular soul—the act or episode by which its quality comes to the test—in which he interests us. With him it is always "a drama of the interior, a tragedy or comedy of the soul, to see thereby how each soul becomes conscious of itself." In the Preface to the later edition of *Sordello*, Mr. Browning himself told us that to him little else seems worth study except the development of a soul, the incidents, the story, of that. And, in fact, the intellectual public generally agrees with him. It is because he has ministered with such marvellous vigour, and variety, and fine skill to this interest, that he is the most modern, to modern people the most important, of poets.

So much for Mr. Browning's matter ; for his manner, we hold Mr. Symons right in thinking him a master of all the arts of poetry. "These extraordinary little poems," says Mr. Symons of "Johannes Agricola" and "Porphyria's Lover"—

"Reveal not only an imagination of intense fire and heat, but an almost finished art—a power of conceiving subtle mental complexities with clearness and of expressing them in a picturesque form and in perfect lyric language. Each poem renders a single mood, and renders it completely."

Well, after all, that is true of a large portion of Mr. Browning's work. A curious, an erudite artist, certainly, he is to some extent an experimenter in rhyme or metre, often hazardous. But in spite of the dramatic rudeness which is sometimes of the idiosyncrasy, the true and native colour of his multitudinous *dramatis personæ*, or monologists, Mr. Symons is right in laying emphasis on the grace, the finished skill, the music, native and ever ready to the poet himself—tender, manly, humorous, awe-stricken —when speaking in his own proper person. Music herself, the analysis of the musical soul, in the characteristic episodes of its development is a wholly new range of poetic subject in which Mr. Browning is simply unique. Mr. Symons tells us :—

"When Mr. Browning was a mere boy, it is recorded that he debated within himself whether he should not become a painter or a musician as well as a poet. Finally, though not, I believe, for a good many years, he decided in the negative. But the latent qualities of painter and musician had developed themselves in his poetry, and much of his finest and very much of his most original verse is that which speaks the language of painter and musician as it had never before been spoken. No English poet before him has ever excelled his utterances on music, none has so much as rivalled his utterances on art. 'Abt Vogler' is the richest, deepest, fullest poem on music in the language. It is not the theories of the poet, but the instincts of the musician, that it speaks. 'Master Hugues of Saxe-Gotha,' another special poem on music, is unparalleled for ingenuity of technical interpretation: 'A Toccata of Galuppi's' is as rare a rendering as can anywhere be found of the impressions and sensations caused by a musical piece; but 'Abt Vogler' is a very glimpse into the heaven where music is born."

It is true that "when the head has to be exercised before the heart there is chilling of sympathy." Of course, so intellectual a poet (and only the intellectual poet, as we have pointed out, can be adequate to modern demands) will have his difficulties. They were a part of the poet's choice of vocation, and he was fully aware of them :—

"Mr. Browning might say, as his wife said in an early preface, I never mistook pleasure for the final cause of poetry, nor leisure for the hour of the poet—as indeed he has himself said, to much the same effect, in a letter printed many years ago: I never pretended to offer such literature as should be a substitute for a cigar or a game at dominoes to an idle man."

"Moreover, while a writer who deals with

easy themes has no excuse if he is not pellucid to a glance, one who employs his intellect and imagination on high and hard questions has a right to demand a corresponding closeness of attention, and a right to say with Bishop Butler, in answer to a similar complaint: 'It must be acknowledged that some of the following discourses are very abstruse and difficult, or, if you please, obscure; but I must take leave to add that those alone are judges whether or no, and how far this is a fault, who are judges whether or no, and how far it might have been avoided —those only who will be at the trouble to understand what is here said, and to see how far the things here insisted upon, and not other things, might have been put in a plainer manner.'"

In Mr. Symons's opinion *Pippa Passes* is Mr. Browning's most perfect piece of work, for pregnancy of intellect, combined with faultless expression in a perfectly novel yet symmetrical outline: and he is very likely right. He is certainly right in thinking *Men and Women*, as they formerly stood, Mr. Browning's most delightful volumes. It is only to be regretted that in the later collected edition of the works those two magical old volumes are broken up and scattered under other headings. We think also that Mr. Symons in his high praise does no more than justice to *The Ring and the Book*. *The Ring and the Book* is at once the largest and the greatest of Mr. Browning's works, the culmination of his dramatic method, and the turning-point more decisively than *Dramatis Personæ* of his style. Yet just here he rightly marks a change in Mr. Browning's manner :—

"Not merely the manner of presentment, the substance, and also the style and versification have undergone a change. I might point to the profound intellectual depth of certain pieces as its characteristic, or, equally, to the traces here and there of an apparent carelessness of workmanship ; or, yet again, to the new and very marked partiality for scenes and situations of English and modern rather than mediæval and foreign life."

Noble as much of Mr. Browning's later work is, full of intellect, alive with excellent passages (in the first volume of the *Dramatic Idyls* perhaps more powerful than in any earlier work); notwithstanding all that, we think the change here indicated matter of regret. After all, we have to conjure up ideal poets for ourselves out of those who stand in or behind the range of volumes on our book-shelves; and our ideal Browning would have for his entire structural type those two volumes of *Men and Women* with *Pippa Passes*.

Certainly, it is a delightful world to which Mr. Browning has given us the key, and those volumes a delightful gift to our age-record of so much that is richest in the world of things, and men, and their works—all so much the richer by the great intellect, the great imagination, which has made the record, transmuted them into imperishable things of art:—

"'With souls should souls have place'—this, with Mr. Browning, is something more than a mere poetical conceit. It is the condensed expression of an experience, a philosophy, and an art. Like the lovers of his lyric, Mr. Browning has renounced the selfish serenities of wild-wood and dream-palace; he has fared up and down among men, listening to the music of humanity, observing the acts of men, and he has sung what he has heard, and he has painted what he has seen. Will the work live? we ask; and we can answer only in his own words—

It lives,
If precious be the soul of man to man."

# IV

## "ROBERT ELSMERE"

28TH MARCH 1888

## "ROBERT ELSMERE"

THOSE who, in this bustling age, turn to fiction not merely for a little passing amusement, but for profit, for the higher sort of pleasure, will do well, we think (after a conscientious perusal on our own part) to bestow careful reading on *Robert Elsmere*. A *chef d'œuvre* of that kind of quiet evolution of character through circumstance, introduced into English literature by Miss Austen, and carried to perfection in France by George Sand (who is more to the point, because, like Mrs. Ward, she was not afraid to challenge novel-readers to an interest in religious questions), it abounds in sympathy with people as we find them, in aspiration towards something better—towards a certain ideal—in a refreshing sense of second thoughts everywhere. The author clearly has developed a remarkable natural aptitude for literature by liberal reading and most patient care in composition—composition in that narrower sense which is concerned with the building of a good sentence ; as also in that wider sense, which ensures, in a work like this, with so many joints, so many currents of interest, a final unity of impression on the part of the reader, and easy transition by him from one to the other. Well-used to works of fiction which tell all they have to tell in one thin volume, we have read Mrs. Ward's three volumes with unflagging readiness. For, in truth, that quiet method of evolution, which she pursues undismayed to the end, requires a certain lengthiness ; and the reader's reward will be in a secure sense that he has been in intercourse with no mere flighty remnants, but with typical forms, of character, firmly and fully conceived. We are persuaded that the author might have written a novel which should have been all shrewd impressions of society, or all humorous impressions of country life, or all quiet fun and genial caricature. Actually she has chosen to combine something of each of these with a very sincerely felt religious interest ; and who will deny that to trace the influence of religion upon human character is one of the legitimate functions of the novel? In truth, the modern "novel of character" needs some such interest, to lift it sufficiently above the humdrum of life; as men's horizons are enlarged by religion, of whatever type it may be—and we may say at once that the religious type which is dear to Mrs. Ward, though avowedly "broad," is not really the broadest. Having conceived her work thus, she has brought a rare instinct for probability and nature to the difficult task of combining this religious motive and all the learned thought it involves, with a very genuine interest in many varieties of average mundane life.

We should say that the author's special ethical gift lay in a delicately intuitive sympathy, not, perhaps, with all phases of character, but certainly with the very varied class of persons represented in these volumes. It may be congruous with this, perhaps, that her success should be more assured in dealing with the characters of women than with those of men. The men who pass before us in her pages, though real and tangible and effective enough, seem, nevertheless, from time to time to reveal their joinings. They are composite of many different men we seem to have known, and fancy we could detach again from the *ensemble* and from each other. And their goodness, when they are good, is—well! a little conventional; the kind of goodness that men themselves discount rather largely in their estimates of each other. Robert himself is certainly worth knowing—a really attractive union of manliness and saintliness, of shrewd sense and unworldly aims, and withal with that kindness and pity the absence of which so often abates the actual value of those other gifts. Mrs. Ward's literary power is sometimes seen at its best (it is a proof of her high cultivation of this power that so it should be) in the analysis of minor characters, both male and female. Richard Leyburn, deceased before the story begins, but warm in the memory of the few who had known him, above all of his great-souled daughter Catherine, strikes us, with his religious mysticism, as being in this way one of the best things in the book :—

"Poor Richard Leyburn! Yet where had the defeat lain?

"'Was he happy in his school life?' Robert asked gently. 'Was teaching what he liked?'

"'Oh! yes, only——' Catherine paused and then added hurriedly, as though drawn on in spite of herself by the grave sympathy of his look, 'I never knew anybody so good who thought himself of so little account. He always believed that he had missed everything, wasted everything, and that anybody else would have made infinitely more out of his life. He was always blaming, scourging himself. And all the time he was the noblest, purest, most devoted——'

"She stopped. Her voice had passed beyond her control. Elsmere was startled by the feeling she showed. Evidently he had touched one of the few sore places in this pure heart. It was as though her memory of her father had in it elements of almost intolerable pathos, as though the child's brooding love and loyalty were in perpetual protest even now after this lapse of years against the verdict which an over-scrupulous, despondent soul had pronounced upon itself. Did she feel that he had gone uncomforted out of life—even by her—even by religion? Was that the sting?"

A little later she gives the record of his last hours:—

"'Catherine! Life is harder, the narrower way narrower than ever. I die'—and memory caught still the piteous long-drawn breath by which the voice was broken—'in much—much perplexity about many things. You have a clear soul, an iron will. Strengthen the others. Bring them safe to the day of account.'"

And then the smaller—some of them, ethically, very small—women; Lady Wynnstay, Mrs. Fleming, Mrs. Thornburgh; above all, Robert's delightful Irish mother, and Mrs. Darcy; how excellent they are! Mrs. Darcy we seem to have known, yet cannot have enough of, rejoiced to catch sight of her capital letter on the page, as we read on. In truth, if a high and ideal purpose, really learned in the school of Wordsworth and among the Westmorland hills which Mrs. Ward describes so sympathetically, with fitting dignity and truth of style, has accompanied the author throughout; no less plain, perhaps more pleasing to some readers, is the quiet humour which never fails her, and tests, while it relieves, the sincerity of her more serious thinking:—

"At last Mrs. Darcy fluttered off, only, however, to come hurrying back with little, short, scudding steps, to implore them all to come to tea with her as soon as possible in the garden that was her special hobby, and in her last new summer-house.

"'I build two or three every summer,' she said; 'now there are twenty-one! Roger laughs at me,' and there was a momentary bitterness in the little eerie face; 'but how can one live without hobbies? That's one—then I've two more. My album—oh, you *will* all write in my album, won't you? When I was young —when I was Maid of Honour'—and she drew herself up slightly—'everybody had albums. Even the dear Queen herself! I remember how she made M. Guizot write in it; something quite stupid, after all. *Those* hobbies—the garden and the album—are *quite* harmless, aren't they? They hurt nobody, do they?' Her voice dropped a little, with a pathetic expostulating intonation in it, as of one accustomed to be rebuked."

Mrs. Ward's women, as we have said, are more organic, sympathetic, and really creative, than her men, and make their vitality evident by becoming, quite naturally, the centres of very life-like and dramatic *groups* of people, family or social ; while her men are the very *genii* of isolation and division. It is depressing to see so really noble a character as Catherine soured, as we feel, and lowered, as time goes on, from the happy resignation of the first volume (in which solemn, beautiful, and entire, and so very real, she is like a poem of Wordsworth) down to the mere passivity of the third volume, and the closing scene of Robert Elsmere's days, very exquisitely as this episode of unbelieving yet saintly biography has been conceived and executed. Catherine certainly, for one, has no profit in the development of Robert's improved gospel. The "stray sheep," we think, has by no means always the best of the argument, and her story is really a sadder, more testing one than his. Though both alike, we admit it cordially, have a genuine sense of the eternal moral charm of "renunciation," something even of the thirst for martyrdom, for those wonderful, inaccessible, cold heights of the *Imitation*, eternal also in their æsthetic charm.

These characters and situations, pleasant or profoundly interesting, which it is good to have come across, are worked out, not in rapid sketches, nor by hazardous epigram, but more securely by patient analysis; and though we have said that Mrs. Ward is most successful in female portraiture, her own mind and culture have an unmistakable virility and grasp and scientific firmness. This indispensable intellectual process, which will be relished by admirers of George Eliot, is relieved constantly by the sense of a charming landscape background, for the most part English. Mrs. Ward has been a true disciple in the school of Wordsworth, and really undergone its influence. Her Westmorland scenery is more than a mere background; its spiritual and, as it were, *personal* hold on *persons*, as understood by the great poet of the Lakes, is seen actually at work, in the formation, in the refining, of character. It has been a stormy day:—

"Before him the great hollow of High Fell was just coming out from the white mists surging round it. A shaft of sunlight lay across its upper end, and he caught a marvellous apparition of a sunlit valley hung in air, a pale strip of blue above it, a white thread of stream wavering through it, and all around it and below it the rolling rain-clouds."

There is surely something of "natural magic" in that! The wilder capacity of the mountains is brought out especially in a weird story of a haunted girl, an episode well illustrating the writer's more imaginative psychological power; for, in spite of its quiet general tenour, the book has its adroitly managed elements of sensation—witness the ghost, in which the average human susceptibility to supernatural terrors takes revenge on the sceptical Mr. Wendover, and the love-scene with Madame de Netteville, which, like those other exciting passages, really furthers the development of the proper ethical interests of the book. The Oxford episodes strike us as being not the author's strongest work, as being comparatively conventional, coming, as they do, in a book whose predominant note is reality. Yet her sympathetic command over, her power of evoking, the genius of places, is clearly shown in the touches by which she brings out the so well-known grey and green of college and garden—touches which bring the real Oxford to the mind's eye better than any elaborate description

—for the beauty of the place itself resides also in delicate touches. The book passes indeed, successively, through distinct, broadly conceived phases of scenery, which, becoming veritable parts of its texture, take hold on the reader, as if in an actual sojourn in the places described. Surrey—its genuine though almost suburban wildness, with the vicarage and the wonderful abode, above all, the ancient library of Mr. Wendover, all is admirably done, the landscape naturally counting for a good deal in the development of the profoundly meditative, country-loving souls of Mrs. Ward's favourite characters.

Well ! Mrs. Ward has chosen to use all these varied gifts and accomplishments for a certain purpose. Briefly, Robert Elsmere, a priest of the Anglican Church, marries a very religious woman ; there is the perfection of "mutual love" ; at length he has doubts about "historic Christianity" ; he gives up his orders ; carries his learning, his fine intellect, his goodness, nay, his saintliness, into a kind of Unitarianism ; the wife becomes more intolerant than ever ; there is a long and faithful effort on both sides, eventually successful, on the part of these mentally divided people, to hold together; ending with the hero's death, the genuine piety and resignation of which is the crowning touch in the author's able, learned, and thoroughly sincere apology for Robert Elsmere's position.

For good or evil, the sort of doubts which troubled Robert Elsmere are no novelty in literature, and we think the main issue of the "religious question" is not precisely where Mrs. Ward supposes—that it has advanced, in more senses than one, beyond the point raised by Renan's *Vie de Jésus*. Of course, a man such as Robert Elsmere came to be ought not to be a clergyman of the Anglican Church. The priest is still, and will, we think, remain, one of the necessary types of humanity; and he is untrue to his type, unless, with whatever inevitable doubts in this doubting age, he feels, on the whole, the preponderance in it of those influences which make for faith. It is his triumph to achieve as much faith as possible in an age of negation. Doubtless, it is part of the ideal of the Anglican Church that, under certain safeguards, it should find room for latitudinarians even among its clergy. Still, with these, as with all other genuine priests, it is the positive not the negative result that justifies the position. We have little patience with those liberal clergy who dwell on nothing else than the difficulties of faith and the propriety of concession to the opposite force. Yes! Robert Elsmere was certainly right in ceasing to be a clergyman. But it strikes us as a blot on his philosophical pretensions that he should have been both so late in perceiving the difficulty, and then so sudden and trenchant in dealing with so great and complex a question. Had he possessed a perfectly philosophic or scientific temper he would have hesitated. This is not the place to discuss in detail the theological position very ably and seriously argued by Mrs. Ward. All we can say is that, one by one, Elsmere’s objections may be met by considerations of the same *genus*, and not less equal weight, relatively to a world so obscure, in its origin and issues, as that in which we live.

Robert Elsmere was a type of a large class of minds which cannot be sure that the sacred story is true. It is philosophical, doubtless, and a duty to the intellect to recognize our doubts, to locate them, perhaps to give them practical effect. It may be also a moral duty to do this. But then there is also a large class of minds which cannot be sure it is false—minds of very various degrees of conscientiousness and intellectual power, up to the highest. They will think those who are quite sure it is false unphilosophical through lack of doubt. For their part, they make allowance in their scheme of life for a great possibility, and with some of them that bare concession of possibility (the subject of it being what it is) becomes the most important fact in the world. The recognition of it straightway opens wide the door to hope and love; and such persons are, as we fancy they always will be, the nucleus of a Church. Their particular phase of doubt, of philosophic uncertainty, has been the secret of millions of good Christians, multitudes of worthy priests. They knit themselves to believers, in various degrees, of all ages. As against the purely negative action of the scientific spirit, the high-pitched Grey, the theistic Elsmere, the "ritualistic priest," the quaint Methodist Fleming, both so admirably sketched, present perhaps no unconquerable differences. The question of the day is not between one and another of these, but in another sort of opposition, well defined by Mrs. Ward herself, between—

"Two estimates of life—the estimate which is the offspring of the scientific spirit, and which is for ever making the visible world fairer and more desirable in mortal eyes; and the estimate of Saint Augustine."

To us, the belief in God, in goodness at all, in the story of Bethlehem, does not rest on evidence so diverse in character and force as Mrs. Ward supposes. At his death Elsmere has started what to us would be a most unattractive place of worship, where he preaches an admirable sermon on the purely human aspect of the life of Christ. But we think there would be very few such sermons in the new church or chapel, for the interest of that life could hardly be very varied, when all such sayings as that "though He was rich, for our sakes He became poor" have ceased to be applicable to it. It is the infinite nature of Christ which has led to such diversities of genius in preaching as St. Francis, and Taylor, and Wesley.

And after all we fear we have been unjust to Mrs. Ward's work. If so, we should read once more, and advise our readers to read, the profoundly thought and delicately felt chapter—chapter forty-three in her third volume—in which she describes the final spiritual reunion, on a basis of honestly diverse opinion, of the husband and wife. Her view, we think, could hardly have been presented more attractively. For ourselves we can only thank her for pleasure and profit in the reading of her book, which has refreshed actually the first and deepest springs of feeling, while it has charmed the literary sense.

# V

# THEIR MAJESTIES' SERVANTS

27TH JUNE 1888

## THEIR MAJESTIES' SERVANTS

*Annals of the English Stage, from Thomas Betterton to Edmund Kean.* By Dr. Doran, F.S.A. Edited and revised by Robert W. Lowe. John C. Nimmo.

THOSE who care for the history of the drama as a branch of literature, or for the history of that general development of human manners of which the stage has been always an element and a very lively measure or *index*, will be grateful to Mr. Lowe for this revised and charmingly illustrated edition of Dr. Doran's pleasant old book. Three hundred years and more of a singularly varied and vivacious sort of history!—it was a bold thing to undertake; and Dr. Doran did his work well—did it with adequate "love." These *Annals of the English Stage, from Thomas Betterton to Edmund*

*Kean*, are full of the colours of life in their most emphatic and motley contrasts, as is natural in proportion as the stage itself concentrates and artificially intensifies the character and conditions of ordinary life. The long story of "Their Majesties' Servants," treated thus, becomes from age to age an agreeable addition to those personal memoirs—Evelyn's, and the like—which bring the influence and charm of a visible countenance to the dry tenour of ordinary history, and the critic's work upon it naturally becomes, in the first place, a mere gathering of some of the flowers which lie so abundantly scattered here and there.

A history of the English stage must necessarily be in part a history of one of the most delightful of subjects—old London, of which from time to time we catch extraordinary glimpses in Dr. Doran's pages. From 1682 to 1695, as if the Restoration had not come, there was but one theatre in London. In Charles I.'s time Shoreditch was the dramatic quarter of London *par excellence*:—

"The popular taste was not only there directed towards the stage, but it was a district wherein many actors dwelt, and consequently died. The baptismal register of St. Leonard's, Shoreditch, contains Christian names which appear to have been chosen with reference to the heroines of Shakespeare; and the record of burials bears the name of many an old actor of mark whose remains now lie within the churchyard."

Earlier and later, the Surrey side of the Thames was the favourite locality for play-houses. The Globe was there, and the Bear-garden, represented in Mr. Lowe's luxurious new edition by delightful woodcuts. For this new edition adds to the original merits of the work the very substantial charm of abundant illustrations, first-rate in subject and execution, and of three kinds—copper-plate likenesses of actors and other personages connected with theatrical history; a series of delicate, picturesque, highly detailed woodcuts of theatrical topography, chiefly the little old theatres; and, by way of tail-pieces to the chapters, a second series of woodcuts of a vigour and reality of information, within very limited compass, which make one think of Callot and the German "little masters," depicting Garrick and other famous actors in their favourite scenes.

In the vignettes of the Bear-garden and the Swan Theatre, for instance, the artist has managed to throw over his minute plate a wonderful air of pleasantness, a light which, though very delicate, is very theatrical. The river and its tiny craft, the little gabled houses of the neighbourhood, with a garden or two dropped in, tell delightfully in the general effect. They are worthy to rank with Cruikshank's illustrations of *Jack Sheppard* and *The Tower of London*, as mementoes of the little old smokeless London before the century of Johnson, though that, too, as Dr. Doran bears witness, knew what fogs could be. Then there is the Fortune Theatre near Cripplegate, and, most charming of all, two views—street and river fronts—the Duke's Theatre, Dorset Garden, in Fleet Street, designed by Wren, decorated by Gibbons—graceful, naïve, dainty, like the work of a very refined Palladio, working minutely, perhaps more delicately than at Vicenza, in the already crowded city on the Thames side.

The portraits of actors and other theatrical celebrities range from Elizabeth, from the melodramatic costumes and faces of the contemporaries of Shakespeare, to the conventional costumes, the rotund expression, of the age of the Georges, masking a power of imaginative impersonation probably unknown in Shakespeare's day. Edward Burbage, like Shakespeare's own portrait, is, we venture to think, a trifle stolid. Field—Nathaniel Field, author of *The Fatal Dowry*, and an actor of reputation—in his singular costume, and with a face of perhaps not quite reassuring subtlety, might pass for the original of those Italian, or Italianized, voluptuaries in sin which pleased the fancy of Shakespeare's age. Mixed up with many striking, thoroughly dramatic physiognomies, it must be confessed that some of these portraits scarcely help at all to explain the power of the players to whom they belonged. That, perhaps, is what we might naturally expect; the more, in proportion as the dramatic art is a matter in which many very subtle and indirect channels to men's sympathy are called into play. Edward Alleyn, from the portrait preserved at his noble foundation at Dulwich, like a fine Holbein, figures, in blent strength and delicacy, as a genial, or perhaps jovial, soul, finding time for sentiment,—Prynne (included, we suppose, in this company, like the skull at the feast) as a likable if somewhat melancholic young man; while Garrick and his wife playing cards, after Zoffany, present a pair of just very nice young people. On the other hand, the tail-pieces, chiefly devoted to Garrick, prove what a wonderful natural variety there was in Garrick's soul, and are well worth comparative study. Noticeable again, among the whole-plate portraits, is the thoroughly reassuring countenance of Steele, the singularly fine heads of John, Charles, and Fanny Kemble, while the certainly plain, pinched countenance of William Davenant reminds one of Charles Kean, and might well have lighted up, as did his, when the soul came into it, into power and charm, as the speaking eyes assure us even in its repose.

The Renaissance inherited the old foolish prejudice of Roman times, when, although the writers of plays were the intimate friends of emperors, the actors were thought infamous.

Still, on the whole, actors fared better in England than in Romanist France, where Molière was buried with less ceremony than a favourite dog. Very different was the treatment of the eminent Mrs. Oldfield, who died in 1730 :—

"Poor 'Narcissa' after death (says Walpole) was attired in a Holland nightdress, with tucker and double ruffles of Brunswick lace, of which latter material she also wore a headdress, and a pair of new kid gloves. In this dress the deceased actress received such honour as actress never received before, nor has ever received since. The lady lay in state in the Jerusalem Chamber. Had she been really a queen the public could not have thronged more eagerly to the spectacle; and after the lying in state there was a funeral of as much ceremony as has been observed at the obsequies of many a queen. There were anthems and prayers and a sermon; and Dr. Parker, who officiated, remarked, when all was over, to a few particular friends, and with some equivocation, as it seems to me, that he 'buried her very willingly, and with much satisfaction.'"

Yet even in England players had need of

powerful protectors. "Wit," said Chesterfield, opposing an unjust licensing Act, "Wit, my lords! is the property of those who have it, and too often the only property they have to depend on." Wit, indeed, with the other gifts that make good company, has largely gone with theatrical talents, too often little to the benefit of the gifted persons. Theatrical society, rather than the theatre, has made the lives of actors as we see them in these volumes, in many cases so tragic, even sordidly tragic.

If misery and madness abound in stage life, so also does an indomitable cheerfulness, always at least a cheerful countenance. Dr. Doran's book abounds, as might be expected, with admirable impromptus and the like; one might collect a large posy of them. Foote, seeing a sweep on a blood-horse, remarked, "There goes Warburton on Shakespeare!" When he heard that the Rockingham Cabinet was fatigued to death and at its wits' end, he exclaimed that it could not have been the length of the journey which had tired it. Again, when Lord Carmarthen, at a party, told him his handkerchief was hanging from his pocket, Foote replaced it with a "Thank you, my lord; you know the company better than I." Jevon, a century earlier, was in the habit of taking great liberties with authors and audience. He made Settle half mad and the house ecstatic when having, as Lycurgus, Prince of China, to "*fall on his sword*," he placed it flat on the stage, and, falling over it, "died," according to the direction of the acting copy. Quaint enough, but certainly no instance of anybody's wit, is the account of how a French translation of a play of Vanbrugh—not architect of Blenheim only, but accomplished in many other ways—appeared at the Odéon, in 1862, with all fitting raptures, as a posthumous work of Voltaire recently discovered. The Voltairean wit was found as "delightful in this as in the last century."

Of Shakespeare on the stage Dr. Doran has a hundred curious things to note:—that Richard the Third, for instance, who has retained a so unflattering possession of the stage, was its "first practically useful patron." We see Queen Elizabeth full of misgiving at a difficult time at the popularity of Richard the Second:—"The deposition and death of King Richard the

Second." "Tongues whisper to the Queen that this play is part of a great plot to teach her subjects how to murder kings." It is perhaps not generally known that Charles Shakespeare, William's brother, survived till the Restoration. Oldys says, *à propos* of the restoration of the stage at that time :—

"The actors were greedily inquisitive into every little circumstance, more especially in Shakespeare's dramatic character, which his brother could relate of him. But he, it seems, was so stricken in years, and possibly his memory so weakened by infirmities, that he could give them but little light into their inquiries ; and all that could be recollected from him of his brother Will in that station was the faint, general, and almost lost ideas he had of having once seen him act a part in one of his own comedies, wherein being present to personate a decrepit old man, he wore a long beard, and appeared so weak and drooping and unable to walk, that he was forced to be supported and carried by another person to a table, at which he was seated among some company who were eating, and one of them sang a song."

This description applies to old Adam in *As You Like It.* Many are the evidences that Shakespeare's reputation had from time to time a struggle to maintain itself. James Howard, in Pepys's day—

"Belonged to the faction which affected to believe that there was no popular love for Shakespeare, to render whom palatable he arranged *Romeo and Juliet* for the stage, with a double *dénouement*—one serious, the other hilarious. If your heart were too sensitive to bear the deaths of the loving pair, you had only to go on the succeeding afternoon to see them wedded, and set upon the way of a well-assured domestic felicity."

In 1678 Rymer asserted (was it undesignedly a true testimony to the acting of his time?) that Shakespeare had depicted Brutus and Cassius as "Jack Puddins."

Here, as in many another detail, we are reminded, of course, of the difference between our own and past times in mimic as in real life. For Prynne one of the great horrors of the stage was the introduction of actresses from France by Henrietta Maria, to take the place of young male actors of whom Dr. Doran has some interesting notices. Who the lady was who first trod the stage as a professional actress is not known, but her part was Desdemona. And yet it was long after that—

"Edward Kynaston died (in 1712). He lies buried in the churchyard of St. Paul's, Covent Garden. If not the greatest actor of his day, Kynaston was the greatest of the 'boy-actresses.' So exalted was his reputation 'that,' says Downes, 'it has since been disputable among the judicious, whether any woman that succeeded him so sensibly touched the audience as he.'"

In Charles II.'s time it was a custom to return the price of admission to all persons who left the theatre before the close of the first act. Consequently, many shabby persons were wont to force their way in without paying, on the plea that they did not intend to remain beyond the time limited. Hence much noisy contention, to the great discomfort even of Royalty. The brawling, drinking habits of the time were even more discomforting. An angry word, passed one April evening of 1682 between the son of Sir Edward Dering and a hot-blooded young

Welshman, led to recrimination and sword-drawing. The two young fellows not having elbow-room in the pit, clambered on to the stage, and fought there, to the greater comfort of the audience, and with a more excited fury on the part of the combatants. The mingling of the public with the players was a practice which so annoyed the haughty French actor, Baron, that to suggest to the audience the absurdity of it, he would turn his back on them for a whole act, and play to the audience on the stage. Sometimes the noise was so loud that an actor's voice would scarcely be heard. It was about 1710 that the word *encore* was introduced at the operatic performances in the Haymarket, and very much objected to by plain-going Englishmen. It was also the custom of some who desired the repetition of a song to cry *Altra volta! Altra volta!*

Even indirectly the history of the stage illustrates life, and affords many unexpected lights on historical characters. Oliver Cromwell, though he despised the stage, could condescend to laugh at, and with, men of less dignity than actors. Buffoonery was not entirely expelled from his otherwise grave court. Oxford and Drury Lane itself dispute the dignity of giving birth to Nell Gwynne with Hereford, where a mean house is still pointed out as the first home of this mother of a line of dukes, whose great-grandson was to occupy the neighbouring palace as Bishop of Hereford for forty years. At her burial in St. Martin's-in-the-Fields, Archbishop Tenison preached the sermon. When this was subsequently made the ground of exposing him to the reproof of Queen Mary, she remarked that the good doctor, no doubt, had said nothing but what the facts authorized.

"Who should act genteel comedy perfectly," asks Walpole, "but people of fashion, that have sense?" And, in truth, the seventeenth century gave many ladies to the stage, Mrs. Barry being the most famous of them. Like many eminent actors, she was famous for the way in which she would utter one single expression in a play. Dr. Doran gives some curious instances from later actors. "What mean my grieving subjects?" uttered in the character of Queen Elizabeth, was invested by her with such emphatic grace and dignity as to call up murmurs of approbation which swelled into thunders of applause. Her noble head is here engraved after Kneller, like the head of a magnificent visionary man.

Should we really care for the greatest actors of the past could we have them before us? Should we find them too different from our accent of thought, of feeling, of speech, in a thousand minute particulars which are of the essence of all three? Dr. Doran's long and interesting records of the triumphs of Garrick, and other less familiar, but in their day hardly less astonishing, players, do not relieve one of the doubt. Garrick himself, as sometimes happens with people who have been the subject of much anecdote and other conversation, here as elsewhere, bears no very distinct figure. One hardly sees the wood for the trees. On the other hand, the account of Betterton, "perhaps the greatest of English actors," is delightfully fresh. That intimate friend of Dryden, Tillotson, Pope, who executed a copy of the actor's portrait by Kneller which is still extant, was worthy of their friendship; his career brings out the best elements in stage life. The stage in these volumes presents itself indeed not merely as a mirror of life, but as an illustration of the utmost intensity of life, in the fortunes and characters of the players. Ups and downs, generosity, dark fates, the most delicate goodness, have nowhere been more prominent than in the private existence of those devoted to the public mimicry of men and women. Contact with the stage, almost throughout its history, presents itself as a kind of touchstone, to bring out the *bizarrerie*, the theatrical tricks and contrasts, of the actual world.

# VI

# WORDSWORTH

27TH FEBRUARY 1889

## WORDSWORTH

*The Complete Poetical Works of William Wordsworth.* With an Introduction by John Morley. Macmillans.

*The Recluse.* By William Wordsworth. Macmillans.

*Selections from Wordsworth.* By William Knight and other Members of the Wordsworth Society. With Preface and Notes. Kegan Paul.

THE appearance, so close to each other, of Professor Knight's careful and elaborately annotated *Selections from William Wordsworth*, of Messrs. Macmillan's collected edition of the poet's works, with the first book of *The Recluse*, now published for the first time, and of an excellent introductory essay by Mr. John Morley, forms a welcome proof that the study of the most philosophic of English poets is increasing among us. Surely nothing could be better, hardly anything more directly fitted than a careful reading of Wordsworth, to counteract the faults and offences of our busy generation, in regard both to thought and taste, and to remind people, amid the enormous expansion, at the present time, of all that is material and mechanical in life, of the essential value, the permanent ends, of life itself. In the collected edition the poems are printed with the dates, so far as can be ascertained, in the order of their composition—an arrangement which has indisputable recommendations for the student of Wordsworth's genius; though the former method of distributing his work into large groups of subject had its value, as throwing light upon his poetic motives, and more especially as coming from himself.

In his introductory essay Mr. Morley has dwelt strongly on the circumstance of Wordsworth's remarkable personal happiness, as having had much to do with the physiognomy of his poetic creation—a calm, irresistible, well-being—almost mystic in character, and yet doubtless connected with physical conditions. Long ago De Quincey noted it as a strongly determinant fact in Wordsworth's literary career, pointing, at the same time, to his remarkable good luck also, on the material side of life. The poet's own flawless temperament, his fine mountain atmosphere of mind (so to express it), had no doubt a good deal to do with that. What a store of good fortune, what a goodly contribution to happiness, in the very best sense of that term, is really involved in a cheerful, grateful, physical temperament; especially, in the case of a poet—a great poet—who will, of course, have to face the appropriate trials of a great poet.

Coleridge and other English critics at the beginning of the present century had a great deal to say concerning a psychological distinction of much importance (as it appeared to them) between the *fancy* and the *imagination*. Stripped of a great deal of somewhat obscure metaphysical theory, this distinction reduced itself to the certainly vital one, with which all true criticism more or less directly has to do, between the lower and higher degrees of intensity in the poet's conception of his subject, and his concentration of himself upon his work. It was Wordsworth who made most of this distinction, assuming it as the basis for the final classification (abandoned, as we said, in the new edition) of his poetical writings. And nowhere is the distinction more realizable than in Wordsworth's own work. For though what may be called professed Wordsworthians, including Matthew Arnold, found a value in all that remains of him —could read anything he wrote, "even the 'Thanksgiving Ode,'—everything, I think, except 'Vaudracour and Julia,'"—yet still the decisiveness of such selections as those made by Arnold himself, and now by Professor Knight, hint at a certain very obvious difference of level in his poetic work.

This perpetual suggestion of an absolute duality between his lower and higher moods, and the poetic work produced in them, stimulating the reader to look below the immediate surface of his poetry, makes the study of Wordsworth an excellent exercise for the training of those mental powers in us, which partake both of thought and imagination. It begets in those who fall in with him at the right moment of their spiritual development, a habit of reading between the lines, a faith in the effect of concentration and collectedness of mind on the right appreciation of poetry, the expectation that what is really worth having in the poetic order will involve, on their part, a certain discipline of the temper not less than of the intellect. Wordsworth meets them with the assurance that he has much to give them, and of a very peculiar kind, if they will follow a certain difficult way, and seems to possess the secret of some special mental illumination. To follow that way is an initiation, by which they will become able to distinguish, in art, speech, feeling, manners, in men and life generally, what is genuine, animated, and expressive from what is only conventional and derivative, and therefore inexpressive.

A very intimate sense of the expressiveness of outward things, which ponders, listens, penetrates, where the earlier, less developed consciousness passed lightly by, is an important element in the general temper of our modern poetry. Critics of literary history have again and again remarked upon it; it is a characteristic which reveals itself in many different forms, but is strongest and most sympathetic in what is strongest and most serious in modern literature; it is exemplified by writers as unlike Wordsworth as the French romanticist poets. As a curious chapter in the history of the human mind, its growth might be traced from Rousseau and St. Pierre to Chateaubriand, from Chateaubriand to Victor Hugo; it has no doubt some obscure relationship to those pantheistic theories which have greatly occupied people's minds in many modern readings of philosophy; it makes as much difference between the modern and the earlier landscape art as there is between the roughly outlined masks of a Byzantine mosaic and a portrait by Reynolds or Romney. Of this new landscape sense the poetry of Wordsworth is the elementary and central exposition; he is more exclusively occupied with its development than any other poet. Wordsworth's own character, as we have already observed, was dominated by a certain contentment, a sort of naturally religious placidity, not often found in union with a poetic sensibility so active as his; and this gentle sense of well-being was favourable to the quiet, habitual observation of the inanimate, or imperfectly animate, world. His life of eighty placid years was almost without what, with most human beings, count for incidents. His flight from the active world, so genially celebrated in this newly published poem of *The Recluse;* his flight to the Vale of Grasmere, like that of some pious youth to the Chartreuse, is the most marked event of his existence. His life's changes are almost entirely inward ones; it falls into broad, untroubled, perhaps somewhat monotonous, spaces; his biographers have very little to tell. What it really most resembles, different as its superficies may look, is the career of those early mediæval religious artists, who, precisely because their souls swarmed with heavenly visions, passed their fifty or sixty years in tranquil, systematic industry, seemingly with no thoughts beyond it. This placid life developed in Wordsworth, to an extraordinary degree, an innate sensibility to natural sights and sounds—the flower and its shadow on the stone, the cuckoo and its echo. The poem of

"Resolution and Independence" is a storehouse of such records; for its fulness of lovely imagery it may be compared to Keats's "Saint Agnes' Eve." To read one of his greater pastoral poems for the first time is like a day spent in a new country; the memory is crowded for a while with its precise and vivid incidents :—

> The pliant harebell swinging in the breeze,
> On some grey rock :
> The single sheep, and the one blasted tree,
> And the bleak music from that old stone wall :—
> In the meadows and the lower ground,
> Was all the sweetness of a common dawn :—
> And that green corn all day is rustling in thine ears !

Clear and delicate at once as he is in the outlining of visible imagery, he is more finely scrupulous still in the noting of sounds; he conceives of noble sound as even moulding the human countenance to nobler types, and as something actually "profaned" by visible form or colour. He has a power likewise of realizing and conveying to the consciousness of his reader abstract and elementary impressions, silence, darkness, absolute motionlessness, or, again, the whole complex sentiment of a particular place, the abstract expression of desolation in the long white road, of peacefulness in a particular folding of the hills.

That sense of a life in natural objects, which in most poetry is but a rhetorical artifice, was, then, in Wordsworth the assertion of what was for him almost literal fact. To him every natural object seemed to possess something of moral or spiritual life, to be really capable of a companionship with man, full of fine intimacies. An emanation, a particular spirit, belonged not to the moving leaves or water only, but to the distant peak arising suddenly, by some change of perspective, above the nearer horizon of the hills, to the passing space of light across the plain, to the lichened Druidic stone even, for a certain weird fellowship in it with the moods of men. That he awakened "a sort of thought in sense" is Shelley's just estimate of this element in Wordsworth's poetry.

It was through nature, ennobled in this way by the semblance of passion and thought, that the poet approached the spectacle of human life. For him, indeed, human life is, in the first instance, only an additional, and as it were incidental grace, upon this expressive landscape.

When he thought of men and women, it was of men and women as in the presence and under the influence of those effective natural objects, and linked to them by many associations. Such influences have sometimes seemed to belittle those who are the subject of them, at the least to be likely to narrow the range of their sympathies. To Wordsworth, on the contrary, they seemed directly to dignify human nature, as tending to tranquillize it. He raises physical nature to the level of human thought, giving it thereby a mystic power and expression; he subdues man to the level of nature, but gives him therewith a certain breadth and vastness and solemnity.

Religious sentiment, consecrating the natural affections and rights of the human heart, above all that pitiful care and awe for the perishing human clay of which relic-worship is but the corruption, has always had much to do with localities, with the thoughts which attach themselves to definite scenes and places. And what is true of it everywhere is truest in those secluded valleys, where one generation after another maintains the same abiding-place; and it was on this side that Wordsworth apprehended religion most strongly. Having so much to do with the recognition of local sanctities, the habit of connecting the very trees and stones of a particular spot of earth with the great events of life, till the low walls, the green mounds, the half-obliterated epitaphs, seemed full of oracular voices, even the religion of those people of the dales appeared but as another link between them and the solemn imageries of the natural world. And, again, this too tranquillized them, by bringing them under the rule of traditional, narrowly localized observances. "Grave livers," they seemed to him under this aspect, of stately speech, and something of that natural dignity of manners which underlies the highest courtesy.

And, seeing man thus as a part of nature, elevated and solemnized in proportion as his daily life and occupations brought him into companionship with permanent natural objects, he was able to appreciate passion in the lowly. He chooses to depict people from humble life, because, being nearer to nature than others, they are on the whole more impassioned, certainly more direct in their expression of passion, than other men; it is for this direct expression of passion that he values their humble words. In much that he said in exaltation of rural life he was but pleading indirectly for that sincerity, that perfect fidelity to one's own inward presentations, to the precise features of the picture within, without which any profound poetry is impossible. It was not for their tameness, but for their impassioned sincerity, that he chose incidents and situations from common life, "related in a selection of language really used by men." He constantly endeavours to bring his language nearer to the real language of men; but it is to the real language of men, not on the dead level of their ordinary intercourse, but in certain select moments of vivid sensation, when this language is winnowed and ennobled by sentiment. There are poets who have chosen rural life for their subject for the sake of its passionless repose; and there are times when Wordsworth himself extols the mere calm and dispassionate survey of things as the highest aim of poetical culture. But it was not for such passionless calm that he preferred the scenes of pastoral life; and the meditative poet, sheltering himself from the agitations of the outward world, is in reality only clearing the scene for the exhibition of great emotions, and what he values most is the almost elementary expression of elementary feelings.

In Wordsworth's prefatory advertisement to the first edition of *The Prelude*, published in 1850, it is stated that that work was intended to be introductory to *The Recluse*: and that *The Recluse*, if completed, would have consisted of three parts. The second part is *The Excursion*. The third part was only planned; but the first book of the first part was left in manuscript by Wordsworth—though in manuscript, it is said, in no great condition of forwardness for the printers. This book, now for the first time printed *in extenso* (a very noble passage from it found place in that prose advertisement to *The Excursion*), is the great novelty of this latest edition of Wordsworth's poetic works. It was well worth adding to the poet's great bequest to English literature. The true student of his work, who has formulated for himself what he supposes to be the leading characteristics of Wordsworth's genius, will feel, we think, a lively interest in putting them to test by the many and various striking passages in what is there presented for the first time.

# VII

# MR. GOSSE'S POEMS

29TH OCTOBER 1890

## MR. GOSSE'S POEMS

*On Viol and Flute.* By Edmund Gosse.

PERHAPS no age of literature, certainly no age of literature in England, has been so rich as ours in excellent secondary poetry; and it is with our poetry (in a measure) as with our architecture, constrained by the nature of the case to be imitative. Our generation, quite reasonably, is not very proud of its architectural creations; confesses that it *knows* too much—knows, but cannot do. And yet we could name certain modern churches in London, for instance, to which posterity may well look back puzzled.—Could these exquisitely pondered buildings have been indeed works of the nineteenth century? Were they not the subtlest creations of the age in which Gothic art was spontaneous? In truth, we have had instances of workmen, who, through long, large, devoted study of the handiwork of the past, have done the thing better, with a more fully enlightened consciousness, with full intelligence of what those early workmen only guessed at. And something like this is true of some of our best secondary poetry. It is the least that is true—the least that can fairly be said in praise of the poetic work of Mr. Edmund Gosse.

Of course there can be no exact parallel between arts so different as architecture and poetic composition. But certainly in the poetry of our day also, though it has been in some instances powerfully initiative and original, there is great scholarship, a large comparative acquaintance with the poetic methods of earlier workmen, and a very subtle intelligence of their charm. Of that fine scholarship in this matter there is no truer example than Mr. Gosse. It is manifested especially in the even finish of his varied work, in the equality of his level—a high level—in species of composition so varied as the three specimens which follow.

Far away, in late spring, "by the sea in the south," the swallows are still lingering around "white Algiers." In Mr. Gosse's "Return of the Swallows," the northern birds—lark and thrush—have long been calling to them :—

> And something awoke in the slumbering heart
> Of the alien birds in their African air,
> And they paused, and alighted, and twittered apart,
> And met in the broad white dreamy square,
> And the sad slave woman, who lifted up
> From the fountain her broad-lipped earthen cup,
> Said to herself, with a weary sigh,
> "To-morrow the swallows will northward fly!"

Compare the following stanzas, from a kind of palinode, "1870-1871," years of the Franco-German war and the Parisian Commune :—

> The men who sang that pain was sweet
> Shuddered to see the mask of death
> Storm by with myriad thundering feet;
> The sudden truth caught up our breath,
> Our throats like pulses beat.
>
> The songs of pale emaciate hours,
> The fungus-growth of years of peace,
> Withered before us like mown flowers;
> We found no pleasure more in these
> When bullets fell in showers.
>
> For men whose robes are dashed with blood,
> What joy to dream of gorgeous stairs,
> Stained with the torturing interlude
> That soothed a Sultan's midday prayers,
> In old days harsh and rude?

For men whose lips are blanched and white,
  With aching wounds and torturing thirst,
What charm in canvas shot with light,
  And pale with faces cleft and curst,
    Past life and life's delight?

And then Mr. Gosse's purely descriptive power, his aptitude for still-life and landscape, is unmistakably vivid and sound. Take, for an instance, this description of high-northern summer :—

The ice-white mountains clustered all around us,
  But arctic summer blossomed at our feet;
The perfume of the creeping sallows found us,
  The cranberry-flowers were sweet.

Below us through the valley crept a river,
  Cleft round an island where the Lap-men lay;
Its sluggish water dragged with slow endeavour
  The mountain snows away.

There is no night-time in the northern summer,
  But golden shimmer fills the hours of sleep,
And sunset fades not, till the bright new-comer,
  Red sunrise, smites the deep.

But when the blue snow-shadows grew intenser
  Across the peaks against the golden sky,
And on the hills the knots of deer grew denser,
  And raised their tender cry,

> And wandered downward to the Lap-men's dwelling,
> We knew our long sweet day was nearly spent,
> And slowly, with our hearts within us swelling,
> Our homeward steps we bent.

"Sunshine before Sunrise!" There's a novelty in that, for poetic use at least, so far as we know, though we remember one fine paragraph about it in *Sartor Resartus*. The grim poetic sage of Chelsea, however, had never seen what he describes: not so Mr. Gosse, whose acquaintance with northern lands and northern literature is special. We have indeed picked out those stanzas from a quiet personal record of certain amorous hours of early youth in that quaint arctic land, Mr. Gosse's description of which, like his pretty poem on Lübeck, made one think that what the accomplished group of poets to which he belongs requires is, above all, novelty of motive, of subject.

He takes, indeed, the old themes, and manages them better than their old masters, with more delicate cadences, more delicate transitions of thought, through long dwelling on earlier practice. He seems to possess complete command of the *technique* of poetry—every form of what may be called *skill of hand* in it; and what marks in him the final achievement of poetic *scholarship* is the perfect balance his work presents of so many and varied effects, as regards both matter and form. The memories of a large range of poetic reading are blent into one methodical music so perfectly that at times the notes seem almost simple. Sounding almost all the harmonies of the modern lyre, he has, perhaps as a matter of course, some of the faults also, the "spasmodic" and other lapses, which from age to age, in successive changes of taste, have been the "defects" of excellent good "qualities." He is certainly not the—

> Pathetic singer, with no strength to sing,

as he says of the white-throat on the tulip-tree,

> Whose leaves unfinished ape her faulty song.

In effect, a large compass of beautiful thought and expression, from poetry old and new, have become to him matter malleable anew for a further and finer reach of literary art. And with the perfect grace of an *intaglio*, he shows, as in truth the minute *intaglio* may do, the faculty of structure, the logic of poetry. "The New Endymion" is a good instance of such sustained power. Poetic scholar !—If we must reserve the sacred name of "poet" to a very small number, that humbler but perhaps still rarer title is due indisputably to Mr. Gosse. His work is like exquisite modern Latin verse, into the academic shape of which, discreet and coy, comes a sincere, deeply felt consciousness of modern life, of the modern world as it is. His poetry, according with the best intellectual instincts of our critical age, is as pointed out recently by a clever writer in the *Nineteenth Century*, itself a kind of exquisite, finally revised criticism.

Not that he fails in originality; only, the graces, inborn certainly, but so carefully educated, strike one more. The sense of his originality comes to one as but an after-thought; and certainly one sign of his vocation is that he has made no conscious effort to be original. In his beautiful opening poem of the "White-throat," giving his book its key-note, he seems, indeed, to accept that position, reasons on and justifies it. Yet there is a clear note of originality (so it seems to us) in the peculiar charm of his strictly personal compositions; and, generally, in such touches as he gives us of the soul, the life, of the nineteenth century. Far greater, we think, than the charm of poems strictly classic in interest, such as the "Praise of Dionysus," exquisite as that is, is the charm of those pieces in which, so to speak, he transforms, by a kind of colour-change, classic forms and associations into those —say! of Thames-side—pieces which, though in manner or subject promising a classic entertainment, almost unaware bring you home.—No! after all, it is not imagined Greece, dreamy, antique Sicily, but the present world about us, though mistakable for a moment, delightfully, for the land, the age, of Sappho, of Theocritus:—

> There is no amaranth, no pomegranate here,
> But can your heart forget the Christmas rose,
> The crocuses and snowdrops once so dear?

Quite congruously with the placid, erudite, quality of his culture, although, like other poets, he sings much of youth, he is often most successful in the forecast, the expression, of the humours, the considerations, that in truth are more proper to old age:—

> When age comes by and lays his frosty hands
> So lightly on mine eyes, that, scarce aware

Of what an endless weight of gloom they bear,  
I pause, unstirred, and wait for his commands.  
When time has bound these limbs of mine with bands,  
And hushed mine ears, and silvered all my hair,  
May sorrow come not, nor a vain despair  
Trouble my soul that meekly girdled stands.

As silent rivers into silent lakes,  
Through hush of reeds that not a murmur breaks,  
Wind, mindful of the poppies whence they came,  
So may my life, and calmly burn away,  
As ceases in a lamp at break of day  
The flagrant remnant of memorial flame.

Euthanasia !—Yet Mr. Gosse, with all his accomplishment, is still a young man. His youthful confidence in the perpetuity of poetry, of the poetical interests in life, creed-less as he may otherwise seem to be, is, we think, a token, though certainly an unconscious token, of the spontaneous originality of his muse. For a writer of his peculiar philosophic tenets, at all events, the world itself, in truth, must seem irretrievably old or even decadent.

Old, decadent, indeed, it would seem with Mr. Gosse to be also returning to the thoughts, the fears, the consolations, of its youth in Greece, in Italy :—

Nor seems it strange indeed
To hold the happy creed
That all fair things that bloom and die
Have conscious life as well as I.

Then let me joy to be
Alive with bird and tree,
And have no haughtier aim than this,
To be a partner in their bliss.

Convinced, eloquent,—again and again the notes of Epicurean philosophy fall almost unconsciously from his lips. With poetry at hand, he appears to feel no misgivings. A large faith he might seem to have in what is called "natural optimism," the beauty and benignity of nature, if let alone, in her mechanical round of changes with man and beast and flower. Her method, however, certainly involves forgetfulness for the individual; and to this, to the prospect of oblivion, poetry, too, may help to brace us, if, unlike so genial and cheerful a poet as Mr. Gosse, we need bracing thereto:—

Now, giant-like, the tall young ploughmen go
Between me and the sunset, footing slow;
My spirit, as an uninvited guest,
Goes with them, wondering what desire, what aim,
May stir their hearts and mine with common flame,
Or, thoughtless, do their hands suffice their soul?

I know not, care not, for I deem no shame
To hold men, flowers, and trees and stars the same,
  Myself, as these, one atom in the whole.

That is from one of those half-Greek, half-English idylls, reminding one of Frederick Walker's "Ploughman," of Mason's "Evening Hymn," in which Mr. Gosse is at his best. A favourite motive, he has treated it even more melodiously in "Lying in the Grass":—

I do not hunger for a well-stored mind,
I only wish to live my life, and find
My heart in unison with all mankind.

My life is like the single dewy star
That trembles on the horizon's primrose-bar,—
A microcosm where all things living are.

And if, among the noiseless grasses, Death
Should come behind and take away my breath,
I should not rise as one who sorroweth;

For I should pass, but all the world would be
Full of desire and young delight and glee,
And why should men be sad through loss of me?

The light is flying; in the silver-blue
The young moon shines from her bright window
    through:
The mowers are all gone, and I go too.

A vein of thought as modern as it is old! More not less depressing, certainly, to our over-meditative, susceptible, nervous, modern age, than to that antiquity which was indeed the genial youth of the world, but, sweetly attuned by his skill of touch, it is the sum of what Mr. Gosse has to tell us of the experience of life. Or is it, after all, to quote him once more, that beyond those ever-recurring pagan misgivings, those pale pagan consolations, our generation feels yet cannot adequately express—

> The passion and the stress
> Of thoughts too tender and too sad to be
> Enshrined in any melody she knows?

# VIII

# FERDINAND FABRE

"Norine." Par Ferdinand Fabre

12th June 1889

# FERDINAND FABRE

## AN IDYLL OF THE CEVENNES

A French novelist who, with much of Zola's undoubted power, writes always in the interest of that high type of Catholicism which still prevails in the remote provinces of France, of that high type of morality of which the French clergy have nobly maintained the ideal, is worth recommending to the more serious class of English readers. Something of the gift of François Millet, whose peasants are veritable priests, of those older religious painters who could portray saintly heads so sweetly and their merely human *protégés* so truly, seems indeed to have descended to M. Ferdinand Fabre. In the *Abbé Tigrane*, in *Lucifer*, and elsewhere, he has delineated, with wonderful power and patience, a strictly ecclesiastical portraiture—

shrewd, passionate, somewhat melancholy heads, which, though they are often of peasant origin, are never by any chance undignified. The passions he treats of in priests are, indeed, strictly clerical, most often their ambitions—not the errant humours of the mere man in the priest, but movements of spirit properly incidental to the clerical type itself. Turning to the secular brothers and sisters of these peasant ecclesiastics, at first sight so strongly contrasted with them, M. Fabre shows a great acquaintance with the sources, the effects, of average human feeling ; but still in contact—in contact, as its conscience, its better mind, its ideal—with the institutions of religion. What constitutes his distinguishing note as a writer is the recognition of the religious, the Catholic, ideal, intervening masterfully throughout the picture he presents of life, as the only mode of poetry realizable by the poor ; and although, of course, it does a greal deal more beside, certainly doing the high work of poetry effectively. For his background he has chosen, has made his own and conveys very vividly to his readers, a district of France, gloomy, in spite of its almonds, its oil and wine, but certainly grandiose. The large towns, the sparse hamlets, the wide landscape of the Cevennes, are for his books what the Rhineland is to those delightful authors, Messrs. Erckmann-Chatrian. In *Les Courbezon*, the French *Vicar of Wakefield*, as Sainte-Beuve declared, with this imposing background, the Church and the world, as they shape themselves in the Cevennes, the priest and the peasant, occupy about an equal share of interest. Sometimes, as in the charming little book we wish now to introduce, unclerical human nature occupies the foreground almost exclusively; though priestly faces will still be found gazing upon us from time to time.

In form, the book is a bundle of letters from a Parisian *littérateur* to the friend of his boyhood, now the *curé* of one of those mountain villages. He is refreshing himself, in the midst of dusty, sophisticated Paris, with memories of their old, delightful existence—*vagabonde*, *libre*, *agreste*, *pastorale*—in their upland valley. He can appeal safely to the aged *curé's* friendly justice, even in exposing delicacies of sentiment which most men conceal :—

"As for you, frank, certain of your own mind, joyous of heart, methinks scarce understanding those whose religion makes their souls tremble instead of fortifying them—you, I am sure, take things by the large and kindly side of human life."

The story our Parisian has to tell is simple enough, and we have no intention of betraying it, but only to note some of the faces, the scenes, that peep out in the course of it.

The gloom of the Cevennes is the impression M. Fabre most commonly conveys. In this book it is rather the cheerful aspect of summer, those upland valleys of the Cevennes presenting then a symphony in red, so to call it—as in a land of cherries and goldfinches; and he has a genial power certainly of making you really feel the sun on the backs of the two boys out early for a long ramble, of old peasants resting themselves a little, with spare enjoyment, ere the end :—

"As we turned a sharp elbow of the stream the aspect of the country changed. It seemed to me entirely red. Cherries in enormous bunches were hanging everywhere over our heads. . . .

"It was a hut, rather low, rather dark. A log of chestnut was smouldering in a heap of ashes. Every object was in its place: the table, the chairs, the plates ranged on the dresser. A fairy, in truth, reigned there, and, by the touch of her wand, brought cleanliness and order on every side.

"'Is it you, Norine?' asked a voice from a dark corner, three steps from the fireplace.

"'Yes, *mon grand*, it is I! The heat was growing greater every moment, and I have taken in the goats.'

"Norine unclosed the window. A broad light spread over the floor of beaten earth, like a white cloth. The cottage was illuminated. I saw an old man seated on a wooden stool in a recess, where an ample serge curtain concealed a bed. He held himself slightly bent, the two hands held forth, one over the other, on the knob of a knotty staff, highly polished. In spite of eighty years, Norine's grandfather—*le grand*, as they say up there—had not lost a hair: beautiful white locks fell over his shoulders—crisp, thick, outspread. I thought of those fine wigs of tow or hemp with which the distaff of our Prudence was always entangled. He was close shaved, after the manner of our peasants; and the entire mask was to be seen disengaged, all its admirable lines free, commanded by a full-sized nose, below which the good, thick lips were smiling, full of kindness. The eyes, however, though still clear and soft in expression, had a certain fixity which startled me. He raised himself. His stature seemed to me beyond proportion. He was really beautiful, with the contentment of his face, straight as the trunk of a chestnut, his old velvet coat thrown back, his shirt of coarse cloth open at the breast, so that one saw the play of the ribs.

"'*Monsieur le neveu!*' he cried; 'where are you! Come to me! I am blind.'

"I approached. He felt me, with ten fingers, laying aside his staff.

"'And you would not take offence if a poor peasant like me embraced you?'

"'Quick, Jalaguier!' I cried, throwing myself into his arms. 'Quick!' He pressed me till the joints started. Leaned upon his broad chest, I heard the beating of his heart. It beat under my ears with a burden like our bell at

Camplong. What powerful vitality in Norine's *grand!* 'It does an old man good:—a good hug!' he said, letting me go."

The boyish visitors are quite ready to sit down there to dinner:—

"With the peasant of the Cevennes (M. Fabre tells us) the meal is what nature meant it to be—a few moments for self-recovery after fatigue, a short space of silence of a quite elevated character, almost sacred. The poor human creature has given the sweat of his brow to extort from an ungrateful soil his daily bread; and now he eats that well-savoured bread in silent self-respect.

"'It is a weary thing to be thinking always of one's work (says the *grand* to the somewhat sparing Norine). We must also think of our sustenance. You are too enduring, my child! it is a mistake to demand so much of your arms. In truth, *le bon Dieu* has cut you out after the pattern of your dead father. Every morning, in my prayers, I put in my complaint thereanent. My poor boy died from going too fast. He could never sit still when it was a question of gathering a few *sous* from the fields; and those fields took and consumed him.'"

The boy fancies that the blind eyes are turned towards a particular spot in the landscape, as if they saw:—

"'I often turn my eyes in that direction (the old man explains) from habit. One might suppose that a peasant had the scent of the earth on which he has laboured. I have given so much of the sweat of my brow—there—towards Rocaillet! Angélique, my dead wife, was of Rocaillet; and when she married me, brought a few morsels of land in her apron. What a state they're in now!—those poor morsels of land we used to weed and rake and hoe, my boy and I! What superb crops of vetches we mowed then, for feeding, in due time, our lambs, our calves! All is gone to ruin since my blindness, and especially since Angélique left me for the churchyard, never to come back.' He paused to my great relief. For every one of those phrases he modulated under the fig-trees more sadly than the Lamentations of Jeremiah on *Jeudi Saint* overset me—was like death."

That is good drawing, in its simple and quiet way! The actual scene, however, is cheerful enough on this early summer day—a symphony, as we said, in cherries and goldfinches, in which the higher valleys of the Cevennes abound. In fact, the boys witness the *accordailles*, the engagement, of Norine and Justin Lebasset. The latter is calling the birds to sing good luck to the event:—

'He had a long steady look towards the fruit-trees, and then whistled, on a note at once extremely clear and extremely soft. He paused, watched awhile, recommenced. The note became more rapid, more sonorous. What an astounding man he was, this Justin Lebasset! Upright, his red beard forward, his forehead thrown back, his eyes on the thick foliage of the cherry-trees, his hands on his haunches, in an attitude of repose, easy, superb, he was like some youthful pagan god, gilded with red gold, on his way across the country—like Pan, if he chose to amuse himself by charming birds. You should have seen the enthusiastic glances with which Norine watched him. Upright—she too, slim, at full height, inclining from time to time towards Justin with a movement of irresistible fascination, she followed the notes of her mate; and sometimes, her lips half opening, added thereto a sigh—something of a sigh, an aspiration, a prayer, towards the goldfinch, withdrawn into the shadows.

"The leaves were shaken in the clear, burning green; and, on a sudden, a multitude of goldfinches, the heads red in the wind, the wings half spread, were fluttering from branch to branch. I could have fancied, amid the quivering of the great bunches of fruit, that they were cherries on the wing. Justin suffered his pipe to die away: the birds were come at his invitation, and performed their prelude."

It is forty years afterwards that the narrator, now a man of letters in Paris, writes to his old friend, with tidings of Justin and Norine:—

"In 1842 (he observes) you were close on fifteen; I scarcely twelve. In my eyes your age made you my superior. And then, you were so strong, so tender, so *amiteux*, to use a word from up there—a charming word. And so God, Who had His designs for you, whereas I, in spite of my pious childhood, wandered on my way as chance bade me, led you by the hand, attached, ended by keeping you for Himself. He did well truly when He chose you and rejected me!"

His finding the pair in the wilds of Paris is an adventure, in which, in fact, a goldfinch again takes an important part—a goldfinch who is found to understand the Cevenol dialect:—

"The goldfinch (escaped from its cage somewhere, into the dreary court of the *Institute*) has seen me: is looking at me. If he chose to make his way into my apartment, he would be very welcome. I feel a strong impulse to try him with that unique patois word, which, whistled after a peculiar manner, when I was a boy never failed to succeed in the mountains of Orb—*Béni! Béni! Viens! Viens!* I dare not! He might take fright and fly away altogether."

In effect, the Cevenol bird, true to call, introduces Norine, his rightful owner, whose husband Justin is slowly dying, Towards the end of a hard life, faithful to their mountain ideal, they have not lost their dignity, though in a comparatively sordid medium:

"As for me, my dear Arribas, I remained in deep agitation, an attentive spectator of the scene; and while Justin and Norine, set both alike in the winepress of sorrow, *le pressoir de la douleur*, as your good books express it, murmured to each other their broken consoling words, I saw them again, in thought, young, handsome, in the full flower of life, under the cherry-trees, the swarming goldfinches, of blind Barthélemy Jalaguier. Ah me! It was thus that, five-and-forty years after, in this dark street of Paris, that festive day was finishing, blessed, in the plenitude of nature, by that august old man, celebrated by the alternate song of all the birds of Rocaillet."

Justin's one remaining hope is to go home to those native mountains, if it may be, with the dead body of his boy, dead "the very morning on which he should have received the tonsure from the hands of Mgr. l'Archevêque," and buried now temporarily at the cemetery of Montparnasse:—

"'Theodore calls me. I saw him distinctly to-night. He gave me a sign. After all said, life is heavy, *sans le fillot*, and but for you it were well to be released from it.' . . .

"I have seen Justin Lebasset die, dear Arribas, and was touched, edified, to the bottom of my soul. God grant, when my hour comes, I may find that calm, that force, in the last struggle with life. Not a complaint! not a sigh! Once only he gave Norine a sorrowful, heartrending look; then, from lips already cold, breathed that one word, 'Theodore!' Marcus Aurelius used to say: 'A man should leave the world as a ripe olive falls from the tree that bore it, and with a kiss for the earth that nourished it.' Well! the peasant of Rocaillet had the beautiful, noble, simple death of the fruit of the earth, going to the common receptacle of all mortal beings, with no sense that he was torn away. Pardon, I pray, my quotation from Marcus Aurelius, who persecuted the Christians. I give it with the same respect with which you would quote some holy writer. Ah! my dear Arribas! not all the saints have received canonization."

It is to the priestly character, in truth, that M. Fabre always comes back for tranquillizing effect ; and if his peasants have something akin to Wordsworth's, his priests may remind one of those solemn ecclesiastical heads familiar in the paintings and etchings of M. Alphonse Legros. The reader travelling in Italy, or Belgium perhaps, has doubtless visited one or more of those spacious sacristies, introduced to which for the inspection of some more than usually *recherché* work of art, one is presently dominated by their reverend quiet : simple people coming and going there, devout, or at least on devout business, with half-pitched voices, not without touches of kindly humour, in what seems to express like a picture the most genial side, midway between the altar and the home, of the ecclesiastical life. Just such interiors we seem to visit under the magic of M. Fabre's well-trained pen. He has a real power of taking one from Paris, or from London, to places and people certainly very different from either, to the satisfaction of those who seek in fiction an escape.

# IX

# THE "CONTES" OF M. AUGUSTIN FILON

16TH JULY 1890

"CONTES DU CENTENAIRE." PAR AUGUSTIN FILON
PARIS: HACHETTE ET CIE.

# THE "CONTES" OF M. AUGUSTIN FILON

## TALES OF A HUNDRED YEARS SINCE

It was a happy thought of M. Filon to put into the mouth of an imaginary centenarian a series of delightfully picturesque studies which aim at the minute presentment of life in France under the old *régime*, and end for the most part with the Revolution. A genial centenarian, whose years have told happily on him, he appreciates not only those humanities of feeling and habit which were peculiar to the last century and passed away with it, but also that permanent humanity which has but undergone a change of surface in the new world of our own, wholly different though it may look. With a sympathetic sense of life as it is always,

M. Filon has transplanted the creations of his fancy into an age certainly at a greater distance from ourselves than can be estimated by mere lapse of time, and where a fully detailed antiquarian knowledge, used with admirable tact and economy, is indeed serviceable in giving reality of effect to scene and character. In truth, M. Filon's very lively antiquarianism carries with it a genuine air of personal memory. With him, as happens so rarely, an intimate knowledge of historic detail is the secret of life, of the impression of life; puts his own imagination on the wing; secures the imaginative cooperation of the reader. A stately age—to us, perhaps, in the company of the historic muse, seeming even more stately than it actually was—it is pleasant to find it, as we do now and again on these pages, in graceful *déshabille*. With perfect lightness of touch, M. Filon seems to have a complete command of all the physiognomic details of old France, of old Paris and its people—how they made a holiday; how they got at the news; the fashions. Did the English reader ever hear before of the beautifully dressed doll which came once a month from Paris to Soho to teach an expectant world of fashion how to dress itself? Old Paris! For young lovers at their windows; for every one fortunate enough to have seen it:—"Qu'il est joli ce paysage du Paris nocturne d'il y a cent ans!" We think we shall best do justice to an unusually pretty book by taking one of M. Filon's stories (not because we are quite sure it is the cleverest of them) with a view to the more definite illustration of his method, therein.

Christopher Marteau was a warden of the corporation of *Luthiers*. He dealt in musical instruments, as his father and grandfather had done before him, at the sign of *Saint Cecilia*. With his wife, his only child Phlipote, and Claude his apprentice, who was to marry Phlipote, he occupied a good house of his own. Of course the disposition of the young people, bred together from their childhood, does not at first entirely concur with the parental arrangements. But the story tells, reassuringly, how—to some extent how sadly—they came heartily to do so. M. Marteau was no ordinary shopkeeper. The various distinguished people who had fingered his *clavecins*, and turned over the folios of music, for half a century past, had left their memories behind them; M. de Voltaire, for instance, who had caressed the head of Phlipote with an aged, skeleton hand, leaving, apparently, no very agreeable impression on the child, though her father delighted to recall the incident, being himself a *demi-philosophe*. He went to church, that is to say, only twice a year, on the Feast of St. Cecilia and on the Sunday when the *Luthiers* offered the *pain bénit*. It was his opinion that everything in the State needed reform except the Corporations. The relations of the husband to his affectionate, satiric, pleasure-seeking wife, who knew so well all the eighteen theatres which then existed in Paris, are treated with much quiet humour. On Sundays the four set forth together for a country holiday. At such times Phlipote would walk half-a-dozen paces in advance of her father and mother, side by side with her intended. But they never talked to each other: the hands, the eyes, never met. Of what was Phlipote dreaming? and what was in the thoughts of Claude?

It happened one day that, like sister and brother, the lovers exchanged confidences. "It is not always," observes Phlipote, whom every one excepting Claude on those occasions sought with admiring eyes—

"'It is not always one loves those one is told to love.'

"'What, have *you*, too, a secret, my little Phlipote?'

"'I *too*, Claude! Then what may be yours?'

"'Listen, Phlipote!' he answered. 'We don't wish to be husband and wife, but we can be friends—good and faithful friends, helping each other to change the decision of our parents.'

"'Were I but sure you would not betray me——'

"'Would you like me to confess first? The woman I love—— Ah! but you will laugh at my folly!'

"'No, Claude! I shall not laugh. I know too well what one suffers.'

"'Especially when love is hopeless.'

"'Hopeless?'

"'Alas! I have never spoken to her. Perhaps never shall!'

"'Well! as for me, I don't even know the name of him to whom my heart is given!'

"'Ah! poor Phlipote!'

"'Poor Claude!'

"They had approached each other. The young man took the tiny hand of his friend, pressing it in his own.

"'The woman I adore is Mademoiselle Guimard!'

"'What! Guimard of the Opera?—the *fiancée* of Despréaux?'"

Claude still held the hands of Phlipote, who was trembling now, and almost on fire at the story of this ambitious love. In return she reveals her own. It was Good Friday. She had come with her mother to the *Sainte Chapelle* to hear Mademoiselle Coupain play the organ and witness the extraordinary spectacle of the *convulsionnaires*, brought thither to be touched by the relic of the True Cross. In the press of the crowd at this exciting scene Phlipote faints, or nearly faints, when a young man comes kindly to their aid. "She is so young!" he explains to the mother, "she seems so delicate!" "He looked at me," she tells Claude—"he looked at me, through his half-closed eyelids; and his words were like a caress" :—

"'And have you seen him no more?' asks Claude, full of sympathy.

"'Yes! once again. He pretended to be looking at the window of the *Little Dunkirk*, over the way, but with cautious glances towards our house. Only, as he did not know what storey we live on, he failed to discover me behind my curtain, where I was but half visible.'

"'You should have shown yourself.'

"'Oh, Claude!' she cried, with a delicious gesture of timidity, of shame.

"So they prattled for a long time; he talking of the great Guimard, she of her unknown lover, scarce listening to, but completely understanding each other.

"'Holloa!' cries the loud voice of Christopher Marteau. 'What are you doing out there?'

"The young people arose. Phlipote linked her arm gaily in that of Claude. 'How contented I feel!' she says; 'how good it is to have a friend—to have you whom I used to detest, because I thought you were in love with me. Now, when I know you can't bear me, I shall be nicely in love with you.' The soft warmth of her arm seemed to pass through Claude, and gave him strange sensations. He resumed naïvely, 'Yes! and how odd it is after all that I am not in love with you. You are so pretty!' Phlipote raised her finger coquettishly, 'No compliments, monsieur. Since we are not to marry each other, it is forbidden to pay court to me!'"

From that day a close intimacy established itself between the formerly affianced pair, now become accomplices in defeating the good intentions of their elders. In long conversations, they talked in turn, or both together, of their respective loves. Phlipote allows Claude entrance to her chamber, full of admiration for its graceful arrangements, its virgin cleanliness. He inspects slowly all the familiar objects daily touched by her, her books, her girlish ornaments. One day she cried with an air of mischief, "If *she* were here in my place, what would you do?" and no sooner were the words uttered than his arms were round her neck. "'Tis but to teach you what I would do were *she* here." They were a little troubled by this adventure.

And the next day was a memorable one. By the kind contrivance of Phlipote herself, Claude gains the much-desired access to the object of his affections, but to his immense disillusion. If he could but speak to her, he fancies he should find the courage, the skill, to bend her. Breathless, Phlipote comes in secret with the good news. The great actress desires some one to tune her *clavecin*:—

"'Papa would have gone; but I begged him so earnestly to take me to the Théâtre Français that he could not refuse; and it is yourself will go this evening to tune the *clavecin* of your beloved.'

"'Phlipote, you've a better heart than I! This morning I saw a gentleman, who resembled point by point your description of the unknown at the *Sainte Chapelle*, prowling about our shop.'

"'And you didn't tell me!'

"Claude hung his head.

"'But why not?' the young girl asks imperiously. 'Why not?'

"'In truth I could hardly say, hardly understand, myself. Do you forgive me, Phlipote?'

"'I suppose I must. So make yourself as smart as you can, to please your goddess.'"

Next day she hears the story of Claude's grievous disappointment on seeing the great actress at home—plain, five-and-forty, ill-tempered. He had tuned the *clavecin* and taken flight.

And now for Phlipote's idol! It was agreed that Whitsunday should be spent at Versailles. On that day the royal apartments were open to the public, and at the hour of High Mass the crowd flowed back towards the vestibule of the chapel to witness what was called the procession of the *Cordons Bleus*. The "Blue Ribbons" were the knights of the Order *Du Saint-Esprit* in their robes of ceremony, who came to range themselves in the choir according to the date of their creation. The press was so great that the parents were separated from the young people. Claude, however, at the side of Phlipote, realized the ideal of a faithful and jealous guardian. The *hallebardes* of the *Suisses* rang on the marble pavement of the gallery. Royalty, now unconsciously presenting its ceremonies for the last time, advanced through a cloud of splendour; but before the Queen appeared it was necessary that all the knights of the order down to the youngest should pass by, slow, solemn, majestic.

They wore, besides their ribbons of blue *moiré*, the silver dove on the shoulder, and the long mantle of sombre blue velvet lined with yellow satin. Phlipote watched mechanically the double file of haughty figures passing before them : then, on a sudden, with a feeble cry, falls fainting into the arms of Claude.

Recovered after a while, under shelter of the great staircase, she wept as those weep whose heart is broken by a great blow. Claude, without a word, sustained, soothed her. A sentiment of gratitude mingled itself with her distress. "How good he is !" she thought.

"It was a pity," says her mother a little later —"a pity you did not see the *Cordons Bleus*. Fancy ! You will laugh at me ! But in one of the handsomest of the Chevaliers I felt sure I recognized the stranger who helped us at the *Sainte Chapelle*, and was so gallant with you."

Philpote did not laugh. "You are deceived, mother !" she said in a faint voice. "Pardi !" cries the father. "'Tis what I always say. Your stranger was some young fellow from a shop."

Two months later the young people receive

the nuptial benediction, and continue the musical business when the elders retire to the country. At first a passionate lover, Claude was afterwards a good and devoted husband. Phlipote never again opened her lips regarding the vague love which for a moment had flowered in her heart: only sometimes, a cloud of reverie veiled her eyes, which seemed to seek sadly, beyond the circle of her slow, calm life, a brilliant but chimeric image visible for her alone.

And once again she saw him. It was in the terrible year 1794. She knew the hour at which the tumbril with those condemned to die passed the windows; and at the first signal would close them and draw the curtain. But on this day some invincible fascination nailed her to her place. There were ten faces; but she had eyes for one alone. She had not forgotten, could not mistake, him—that pale head, so proud and fine, but now thin with suffering; the beautiful mobile eyes, now encircled with the signs of sorrow and watching. The convict's shirt, open in large, broad folds, left bare the neck, delicate as a woman's, and made for that youthful face an aureole, of innocence, of martyrdom. His looks met hers. Did he recognize her? She could not have said. She remained there, paralyzed with emotion, till the moment when the vision disappeared.

Then she flung herself into her chamber, fell on her knees, lost herself in prayer. There was a distant roll of drums. The man to whom she had given her maiden soul was gone.

"Cursed be their anger, for it was cruel!" says the reader. But Monsieur Filon's stories sometimes end as merrily as they begin; and always he is all delicacy—a delicacy which keeps his large yet minute antiquarian knowledge of that vanished time ever in service to a direct interest in humanity as it is permanently, alike before and after '93. His book is certainly one well worth possessing.

THE END